AMAZING STORIES

DAVID THOMPSON

AMAZING STORIES

DAVID THOMPSON

The Epic Expeditions of a Great Canadian Explorer

HISTORY/BIOGRAPHY

by Graeme Pole

"This country is geology by day and astronomy by night."
John Boynton Priestley

PUBLISHED BY ALTITUDE PUBLISHING CANADA LTD.
1500 Railway Avenue, Canmore, Alberta T1W 1P6
www.altitudepublishing.com
1-800-957-6888

First published 2003
Reprinted 2004

Publisher	Stephen Hutchings
Associate Publisher	Kara Turner
Editor	Megan Lappi
Digital photo colouring & maps	Scott Manktelow

We acknowledge the financial support of the Government of Canada through the Book Publishing Industry Development Program (BPIDP) for our publishing activities.

Altitude GreenTree Program
Altitude Publishing will plant twice as many trees as were used in the manufacturing of this product.

National Library of Canada Cataloguing in Publication Data

Pole, Graeme, 1956-
David Thompson / Graeme Pole.

(Amazing stories)
Includes bibliographical references.
ISBN 1-55153-972-1

1. Thompson, David, 1770-1857. 2. Explorers--Canada--Biography. 3. Cartographers--Canada--Biography. I. Title. II. Series: Amazing stories (Canmore, Alta.)

FC3212.1.T46P64 2003 971.03'092 C2003-905479-9

Printed and bound in Canada by Friesens
2 4 6 8 9 7 5 3

Contents

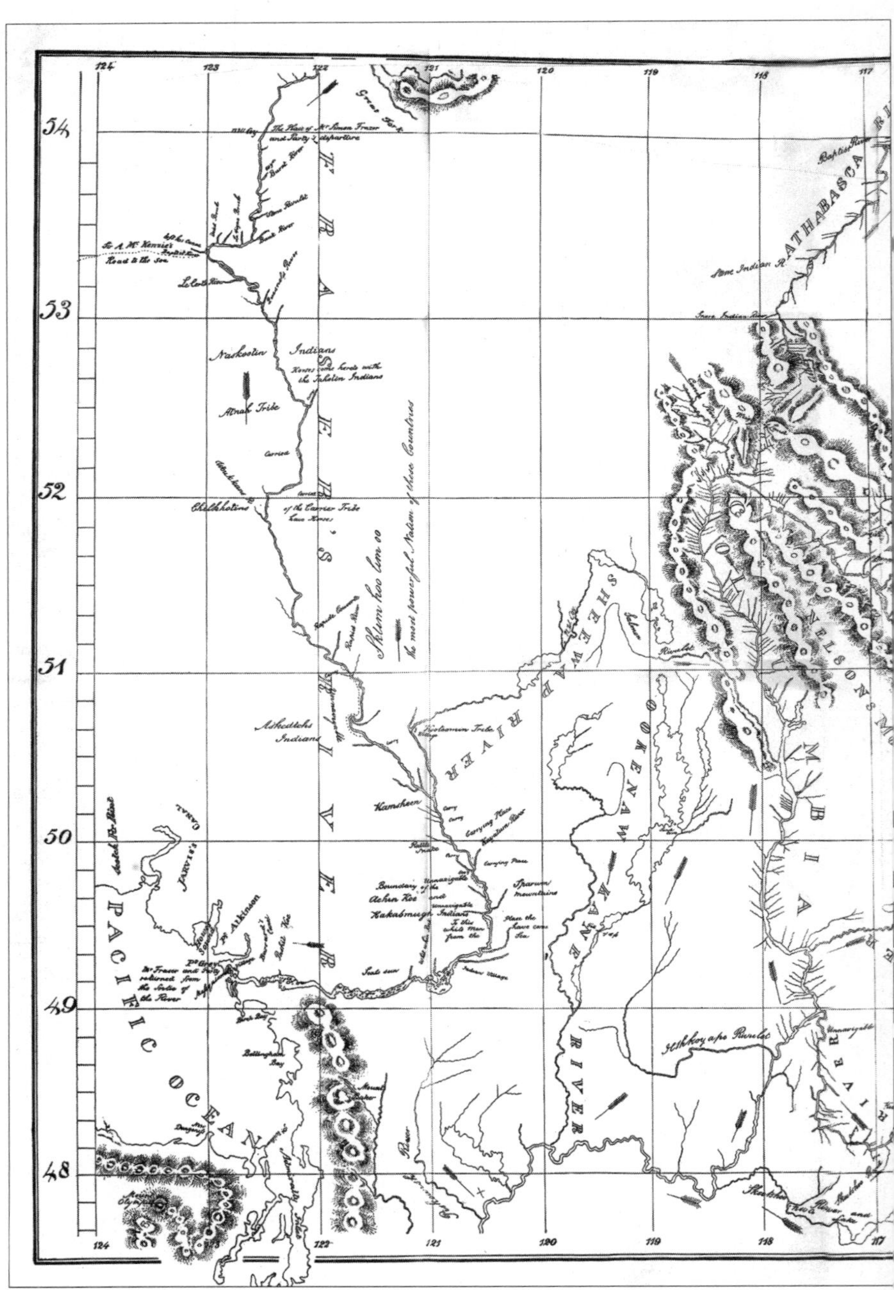

Detail of the Columbia River area from David Thompson's map of 1814
(Reproduced from tracing of original, copyright Francis P. Harper, 1896)

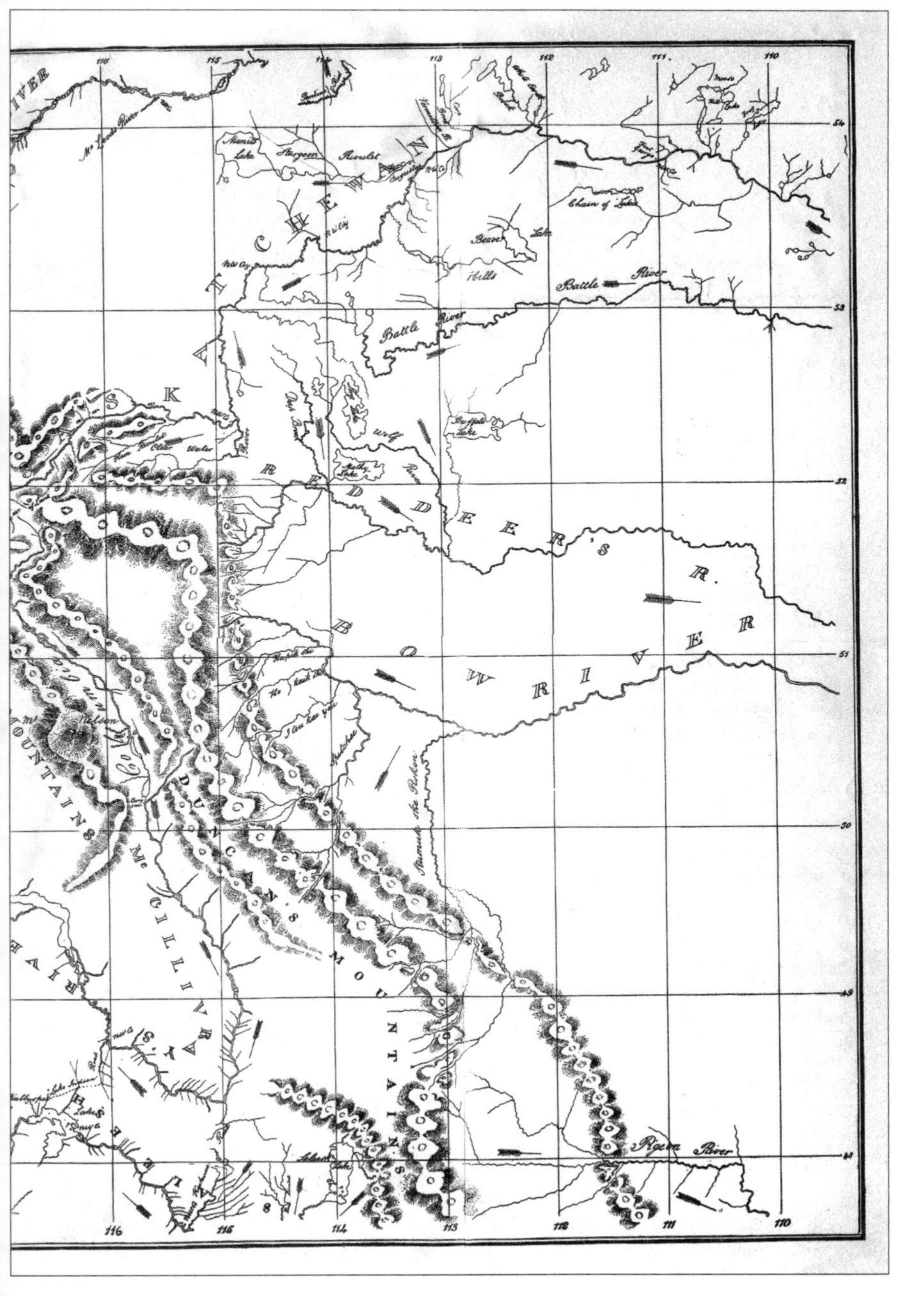

Manito Lake
Sturgeon Rivulet
Chain of Lakes
Beaver Lake
Hills
Battle River
Battle River
Buffalo Lake
RED DEER'S R.
BOW RIVER
Mt Nelson
DUNCAN'S MOUNTAINS
Mc GILLIVRAY'S
Pigeon River
116
115
114
113
112
111
110
54
53
52
51
50
49
48

Prologue

The day began as had many on the journey, with a gale and with snow. As David Thompson and his ragged party crested the height of Athabasca Pass in the Rocky Mountains, the afternoon cleared. The completion of the climb should have been cause for celebration, but as he looked at the men, Thompson could find no cheer. It was January 10, 1811. His voyageurs were dispirited. They were accustomed to wintering in the relative comfort of fur trade outposts, not to sleeping on the snow on a single blanket that on alternate nights was either sodden or frozen.

The westbound brigade had been on the move since late October, covering some 400 kilometres through forest, muskeg, and along rivers. When not travelling, the men had been kept busy building an outpost on the Athabasca River, and making sleds and snowshoes to use in this crossing of the mountains. They had eaten only meat, and lots of it — dried pemmican, or fresh bison and deer, though more often the fare had been desperate — horse, dog, and porcupine.

After scouting ahead to view the beginning of the route down the western slope of the Rockies, Thompson returned to the Pass to find his men plumbing the depths of the snow with a six-metre long section of tree. The probe did not reach bottom. At nightfall the group crowded around a pathetic fire, kindled from the few pieces of wood they had packed from below treeline. The flames gave only enough warmth to melt the snow nearby, into which the logs soon sputtered and sank. The men stumbled off to sleep in the drifts.

The next day, they would begin a descent into the unknown. The Columbia River lay ahead, somewhere, and at its mouth was Thompson's goal — the Pacific Ocean. As he drifted off to sleep, the surveyor must have wondered: for every step through the snow, for every rapid on that river, and for every grinding portage ahead, would his men be fit for the journey?

Chapter 1
The Boy on the Bay

David Thompson was only 14 when he disembarked from the Hudson's Bay Company vessel, *Prince Rupert,* at Churchill Factory on the southwest shore of Hudson Bay. It was September 1784. Whatever meagre comforts the boy had known in England soon seemed royal compared to those of his new home. Thompson described his austere lodgings in his *Narrative,* the record of his life in the wilderness written some 65 years later.

> *A small room was allotted to me without the least article of furniture but a hard bed for the night. My fellow clerks were in the same situation. They were not comfortable but resigned, and I had to become so.*

It took 10 days to unload the supplies from the boat and to reload it with the year's take of furs. It was not until he had helped complete these tasks that the remoteness of Thompson's situation registered.

> *While the ship remained at anchor, from my parent* [mother] *and friends* [it] *appeared* [that I] *was only a few weeks' distance, but when the ship sailed and from the top of the rocks I lost sight of her, the distance became immeasurable, and I bid a long and sad goodbye to my noble, my sacred country, an exile for ever.*

David Thompson came to Hudson Bay in a manner typical of the time. He was born in England to Welsh parents. When he was seven, his widowed mother placed him in a charity school, where the lessons, particularly mathematics, were to prepare him for work in the Royal Navy. After the American Revolution ended, the navy had no immediate need for new sailors, so Thompson and his classmates were readied to enter the merchant marine. He was one of two students recommended by the school to the Hudson's Bay Company (HBC) when it came knocking in the spring of 1784. Rather than face a life in the wilds of Rupert's Land, as central Canada was then known, the other candidate ran away. So Thompson won the posting — a seven-year apprenticeship at the rate of £6 per year.

The HBC could have landed no finer a prospect. The job of apprentice clerk, to which Thompson was assigned, was to assist the governor of a fur trade fort, and to record all matters related to commerce. Thompson, meticulous and orderly, was more than up to the duties. But it seems that the HBC provided little work that first winter. Thompson complained to the fort's governor, Samuel Hearne, that he would lose his ability to write for lack of practice.

Hearne countered by giving Thompson an assignment, but it was not official work. He had Thompson transcribe part of a manuscript that later would become a famous volume in the annals of exploration, called *A Journey to a Northern Ocean.* At the time, Hearne was the most celebrated of the HBC's exploring traders. It is easy to speculate that this brief association had an impact on Thompson. Certainly, the long winter nights in the confines of Fort Churchill would have provided ample time for him to dream of making his own exploratory journeys. Besides his unofficial work for Hearne, Thompson claimed that the only other thing he wrote that winter was a solitary invoice.

Life was hard at Fort Churchill. By the time Thompson arrived at the outpost, HBC traders had already occupied its various incarnations for 70 years. In that interval, they had burned most of the easily available wood, their desire for heat outstripping the ability of the land to provide replacement trees. Thompson described this frigid existence.

> *All of our movements more, or less, were for self-preservation: all the wood that could be collected for fuel, gave us only one fire in the morning, and another in the evening. The rest of the day, if bad weather, we had*

to walk in the guard room with our heavy coats of dressed beaver ...

The interior of the walls of the houses were covered with rime to the thickness of four inches [10 cm], pieces of which often broke off, to prevent which we wetted the whole extent, and made it a coat of ice, after which it remained firm and added to the warmth of the house. The cold is so intense that everything in a manner is shivered by it; continually the rocks are split with a sound like the report of a gun ...

When the HBC ship arrived in September 1785, it carried orders for Thompson to relocate to York Factory. As the next closest outpost to Churchill, it straddled a marshy spit between the Hayes and Nelson rivers, 240 kilometres to the south. The company supplied minimal assistance for the move — a blanket and a boat ride across the mouth of the Churchill River. In the company of two "Packet Indians" — Native people who carried mail between the fur trade forts — Thompson at first walked, and then paddled the muddy shore of Hudson Bay for two weeks. The trio lived on ducks and geese, dodging polar bears all the way.

The Indian rule is to walk past them with a steady step without seeming to notice them.

York Factory was just barely an improvement over Churchill. A clerk who lived there in 1846 called it, "a monstrous blot on a swampy spot." Much of Thompson's account of the following winter described the weather and the changing of the seasons, and how the men fished, and hunted ducks, geese, grouse, cranes, hares, and ptarmigan. Here, Thompson also recounted one aspect of his adjustment to life in the wilds.

> *Accustomed to march in all weathers, I had acquired a power over my eyelids to open, or contract them as circumstances required, and to admit only the requisite quantity of light to guide me, and thus prevented the painful effects of snow blindness.*

Thompson had already developed three skills that would serve him well in his subsequent explorations: he could hunt and fish, he could make a long journey through uncharted terrain, and he could travel in harsh conditions.

A Brief History

David Thompson had arrived on Hudson Bay at a difficult time for the HBC. For almost 120 years, the company had employed a successful if lazy method of trade with the Native peoples. The HBC operated three forts or "factories" at the mouths of major rivers on Hudson Bay, at which its traders waited for Native peoples to deliver furs. Its only inland foray, that of Henry Kelsey in 1690, had not been to establish outposts, but to entice more Native peoples to make the trek to the Bay. The HBC men were gainfully employed for but a few weeks each year, baling the furs and tending to the annual supply ship. As Joseph Robson, an employee turned renegade, commented in 1752, the HBC, "for eighty years slept at the edge of a frozen sea."

It was an arrangement ripe for disruption. By the 1760s, the HBC traders began to feel the effects of the industry of "Canadian peddlers," or independent traders — many of whom were Scots — based at Montréal. Using overland and canoe routes established by Native peoples and developed by French explorers early in the 17th century, the Montréal merchants broached the lands south and west of Hudson Bay, intercepting furs destined for the HBC forts by cutting deals on the spot. It was a commerce akin to guerrilla warfare. The upstarts siphoned away furs and profits that the HBC, by authority of its Royal Charter, considered its own. David Thompson remarked that, in 1786, "the whole of the furs collected at Churchill barely loaded the ships long boat"— the craft used to ferry freight to and from the supply vessel.

The Montréal merchants were at a tremendous disadvantage when compared to the HBC. The prime trading areas of the time, located in what is now Manitoba and Saskatchewan, were eight to ten weeks travel by canoe from Montréal, but were scarcely two weeks travel from the HBC's factories on Hudson Bay. But the incentive for commerce was great — the eastern fur-bearing areas were over-trapped and the Canadian peddlers plunged into the western trade with gusto. Reluctant to change, the HBC continued its old ways long after its trading halls were empty.

Initially, the Canadian traders were ruthless with each other. Although they collectively clobbered the HBC, the

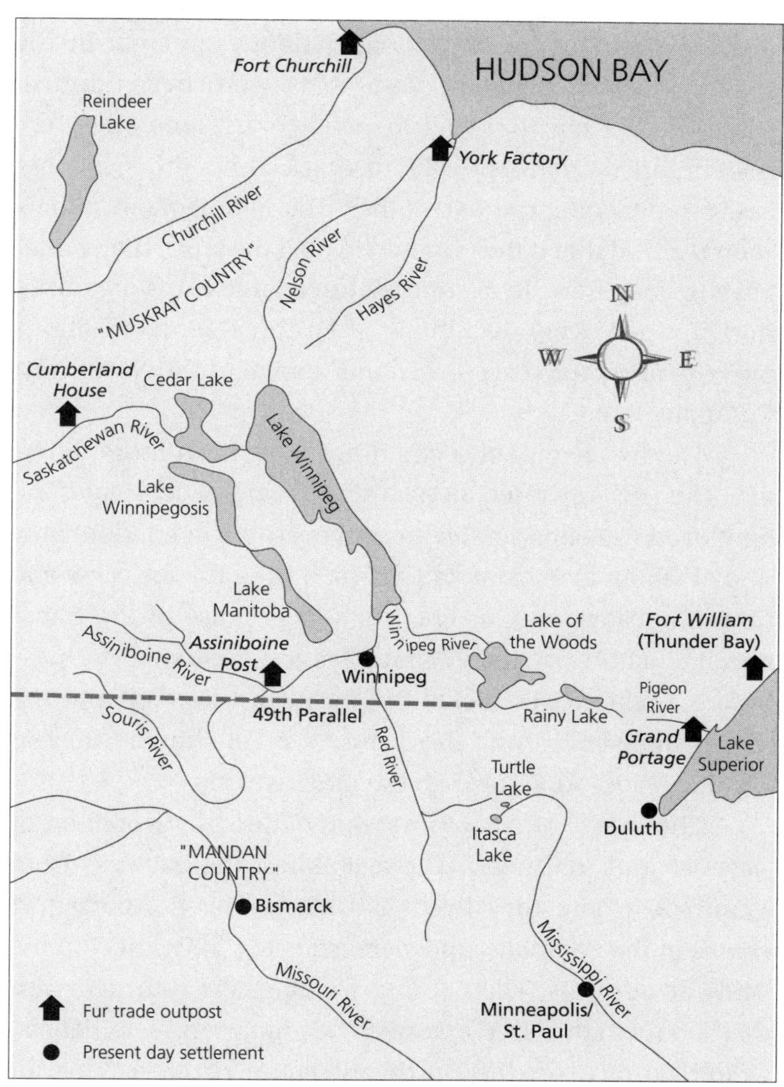

Hudson Bay, the Muskrat Country, and the source of the Mississippi River; 1784–1798

profit margins of the individual traders were slim. In the space of a few decades, vast areas were over-trapped. Disputes over territory lead to violence. In some cases, the traders enticed Native peoples to attack competitors; in other cases traders attacked each other. The independent traders soon realized that if they wanted to oust the HBC, they would have to cooperate. In an uneasy truce, nine firms organized in 1779 into what would — after three reorganizations over the next four years — become known as the North West Company (NWC).

The two companies could not have been more different. The HBC operated along a strict chain of command. All employed were answerable to the governors in London, only one of whom ever came to Canada during the fur trade era. Communication was in English, and because of the trans-oceanic nature of the communication, years might pass before a matter was sorted out between Churchill and the higher-ups at Hudson's Bay House, on Fenchurch Street in London. Promotion through the ranks was slow.

The NWC was a more democratic consortium of "agents" and "partners." The agents ran the business from Montréal, where they lived like kings. The partners held shares in the company, and were expected to "winter" in the wilds at outposts. Each spring the partners returned with their booty to the NWC's western headquarters — initially at Grand Portage on the northwest shore of Lake Superior (about 65 kilometres southwest of the present city of

Thunder Bay) — where they handed over the furs to the eastern brigades, from whom they picked up trading supplies for the following year. Although most of the agents and many of the partners were Scottish, the NWC carried out its business in Québecois French, the language spoken by most of the men who paddled its canoes.

In 1774, early in the rise of the Montréal traders, the HBC responded to the inland challenge by building a post at Pine Island on the Saskatchewan River. Cumberland House did a brisk trade. But affairs of a greater scope intervened, creating a huge setback for the HBC's expansion plans. In 1782, the French Navy captured and razed York Factory and Fort Churchill. It was 1786 before the HBC could build two more posts, farther inland than Cumberland House. In that brief interval, with free run of the country, the Montréal traders became dominant well into the Athabasca Country of what is now northern Alberta.

When the HBC renewed its commitment to moving men inland in the late 1780s, it found that it lacked the manpower to construct and to staff a chain of posts, while also keeping open the forts on Hudson Bay. Most of its workers were Scots from the Orkney Islands. Although accustomed to a harsh climate, and formidable mariners, the men were hopeless in freshwater canoes. The HBC could not entice the Chipewyan and Cree to run the canoes because they would have eliminated themselves as middlemen by doing so. Wherever the HBC did manage to build a trading post, traders of the NWC soon arrived to set up shop. Soon, the NWC was on its way to controlling more than three-quarters of the Canadian fur trade. Such was the backdrop when, in the summer of 1786, David Thompson, a 16-year-old boy on the Bay, was dispatched inland to help promote the HBC's interests.

Chapter 2
Squinting at the Stars

ith 43 other HBC men, David Thompson set off upstream from York Factory along the Hayes River in July 1786. The journey began easily enough, but soon degenerated into the typical grind of the fur trade river rat — a string of mishaps separated by brutal toil.

> *The current could not be stemmed by paddles and two men from each canoe went on shore and took the tracking line, leaving one man to steer the canoe. Although the whole weight of the cargo and baggage did not exceed 800 pounds yet it required a strong steady pull to advance two miles an hour ... The labour is not more than common, but rendered almost dreadful by the*

torment of musketoes [mosquitoes].

Thompson did not complain. With each dip of the paddle and each tug at the tracking line, he put distance between himself and the overbearing feudalism of life at the HBC forts. His heart and his mind opened to the new country around him. David Thompson was falling in love with the Canadian wilderness.

After skirting along the windy north shore of Lake Winnipeg, the brigade portaged into the Saskatchewan River, whose current they fought by poling and lining the canoes. At the forks of the Saskatchewan, the party split. Thompson was in a group of five canoes that followed the South Saskatchewan River a short distance upstream to where the men built South Branch House, just 70 metres from the outposts of the NWC and an independent rival. Here, Thompson recorded his first description of the voyageurs, the Québecois paddlers of the NWC canoes — men with whom he would later spend more than 15 years in the fur trade.

> *The men were all French Canadians, with long red or blue caps, half of which hung down the head; they wore grey capots, or blanket coats belted round their waist, their trousers of grey cloth or dressed leather, and their shoes of the same.*

South Branch House was on the Prairies and Thompson appreciated the dramatic adjustment from life on Hudson Bay. The meat of bison and elk offered a welcome change from the fare of fish and fowl that prevailed at the HBC coastal forts. Travel was easier. Thompson became proficient on horseback, and sometimes ventured 80 kilometres from the outpost to make contact with the Native peoples who supplied the furs and meat to the traders. The young Englishman became acquainted with trading etiquette, and learned the languages of the Cree and Stoney (Assiniboine) peoples.

The following spring, Thompson assisted as the men built a wooden press in which they compacted the winter's take of beaver pelts into bales. After the spring breakup, Thompson and the others headed downstream with the furs. The young trader stopped at Cumberland House on the Saskatchewan River, where he spent the summer.

When the canoes returned from Hudson Bay a few months later, Thompson was summoned to Manchester House on the North Saskatchewan River. He arrived there to discover he would be accompanying a party overland to the southwest, to winter with a group of Piikani (Peigan), on the Bow River, near the present site of Calgary. For a month, Thompson walked across the Prairies, leading a horse that carried his gear.

Of the many themes that play through Thompson's *Narrative*, one dominates: hunger. Whatever the trials of life at the forts on the Bay, the men always had food because they had a great deal of idle time in which to hunt and fish. But in the life of a trader on the move, Thompson discovered that food had to be taken at every opportunity.

Our [Native] guide was utterly at a loss to account for the destitute state of the country where he had so often been in danger of being run over by herds of bisons. Of the few that we saw, we now and then contrived to kill a bull, who would rather fight than run away, but their flesh when boiled is so very tough that although our teeth were in good order, and well inclined to do their duty from having had twenty four hours rest, had we masticated the meat by medical rules it would have taken three hours to make out supper. As it was we gave each mouthful two or three hearty nips, and swallowed it down.

Not far from the destination Thompson struggled to grasp a new detail in the landscape.

The Rocky Mountains came in sight like shining white clouds in the horizon ... as we proceeded they rose in height, their immense masses of snow appeared above the clouds and formed an impassable barrier, even to the eagle.

That winter and the following spring, Thompson shared the tent of an elder named Saukamappee, a Cree who had come to live among the Piikani in his youth. Thompson's record of his talks with Saukamappee — although written more than 60 years later — is one of the early transcriptions of a Native oral history. Saukamappee described three pivotal events: the arrival of horses and muskets on the Plains in about 1730, and the smallpox epidemic of the early 1780s.

While wintering with the Piikani, Thompson met their war chief, Kootanae Appee, "a noble specimen of the Indian warrior of the great plains." The young trader committed a phenomenal gaffe at their greeting, extending his right hand, a gesture that to the Piikani and to other Nitsitapi (Blackfoot peoples) was considered an invitation to fight. Kootanae Appee laughed off the blunder, considering Thompson harmless. Perhaps sensing that their paths would cross again, Saukamappee requested that Kootanae Appee protect Thompson. The chief agreed and, according to Thompson's version of later events, would make good on that promise.

In the spring of 1788, Thompson bid farewell to his Cree host. He and the others returned to Manchester House with a haul of beaver, wolf, and fox pelts. His duties as clerk consumed the summer and autumn, and indeed his life may have continued in the relative tedium of fur trade grunt work had not fate intervened. On December 23, while hauling a sled loaded with meat, Thompson slipped down a riverbank, fracturing his right femur in the fall. The accident happened almost two kilometres from Manchester House. By the time his fellow workers noticed him missing, found him, and brought him home, his leg was severely swollen. Of the injury, his supervisor wrote that he, "put splinters around it with bandages in the best manner I could but such accidents would require a more skillful person than I am."

In Thompson's time, such a grave injury in such a remote location was, if not fatal, certain to be crippling. For three weeks, co-workers kept watch over him day and night. It was more than three months before Thompson was able to get out of bed, and another five months before he could use crutches. When the eastbound brigade departed for York Factory, Thompson was sent along, probably with the intent to have him shipped off to hospital in England. But the journey was so painful and awkward, the injured clerk was unloaded from the canoe at Cumberland House, the next post downstream. There, Thompson languished in a bed in a warehouse until the end of August.

Thompson later wrote that the injury, "by the mercy of God was the best thing that ever happened to me." It was indeed fortuitous that Thompson's final convalescence was at Cumberland House, for on October 7, 1789, Philip Turnor, the HBC's official surveyor and astronomer, arrived to winter at the post. The immediate effect of Turnor's presence was to inspire Thompson to begin keeping a journal, the first entry of which he made just three days after Turnor's arrival. It was the beginning of a ritual that would see Thompson fill 77 notebooks over the next 38 years.

The records of his western travels, probably the most detailed field notes ever made by an explorer over such a length of time, are a mother lode of information for historians. With brevity yet with a tremendous degree of accuracy, the texts paint a vivid portrait of western North America two centuries ago. They were Thompson's prompts when he wrote his *Narrative,* a work that is particularly interesting for its descriptions — sometimes accurate, sometimes fanciful — of various natural processes unrelated to surveying or to commerce, but evidence of a curious intellect: how a mosquito bites its victim, (Thompson watched under a magnifying glass as one took his own blood); how whitewater rapids consist mostly of air; how snow-blindness affects those blue-eyed and grey-eyed more than those brown-eyed; how the now-extirpated herds of plains bison moved north in the autumn and south in the summer; how the eye of the observer tricks the ear into thinking it can hear the aurora borealis; how, of all the migratory waterbird species, only the tundra swan is ever frozen into marshes; and on, and on.

In the 18th century, surveying was called "practical astronomy." Thompson had been educated in the basics. To reward his scholarship, his school gave him a surveying quadrant and navigation books. He had brought these from England but had been obliged to leave them at Churchill because, "my blankets, my gun and my ammunition was a load enough for me to carry [for the] one hundred and fifty miles of mud and marsh to York Factory." Now, in the personage of Turnor, along came a master who was willing to impart his comprehensive knowledge to the keen youngster, who would lend him the necessary instruments, and who would "re-awaken" the mathematician within him.

Navigation, the fixing of a position on the earth's surface, involves two principal elements: the determinations of latitude and longitude. Latitude, the distance north or south of the equator was relatively easy to ascertain in Thompson's time. A surveyor used a sextant to measure the elevation above the horizon, of the sun, a planet, or a known nighttime star. This was done at the moment of its transit — when it reached its maximum elevation above the horizon. For this latter detail, the surveyor required a pocket watch set accurately to local time. When the sun was the object, the process was called a "noon sight." After consulting relevant tables and making some calculations, the surveyor produced the figure for latitude.

Determining longitude, the distance west of the prime meridian at Greenwich, England, was problematic. The measurement was based on a comparison of exact local time with Greenwich mean time. To accomplish this, the surveyor required two watches set to the appropriate times. At a specific instant, he had to measure the angle of the moon relative to the sun, or more likely, to a pair of nighttime stars. This measurement was corrected to account for refraction of the atmosphere, and was then extrapolated through a torturous process of trigonometry, using values and formulas derived from two published sources: the *Nautical Almanac* and its accompanying *Tables Requisite.* A typical computation of this "method of lunar distances," as it was known, required three hours. Thompson was fortunate to have Philip Turnor as a tutor. The senior surveyor was one of the compilers of the *Nautical Almanac.*

Clear weather was essential to all this, as was having the

moon visible. Even though he was not required to make observations in the dead of night, the surveyor was frequently awake until dawn rendering the ensuing calculations. In winter, he would have to continually thaw ink; in summer, swat bugs. The rigors of surveying the Canadian wilds in 1789 were a recipe to put off any but those obsessed. As Philip Turnor soon discovered, Thompson was passionately obsessed.

By early spring 1790, Thompson had taken 41 astronomical fixes at Cumberland House, and, after averaging them, felt competent to record the first description of the outpost's latitude and longitude. His reckoning put the dwelling place only 2.4 kilometres south of, and 4.35 kilometres east of, where today's surveyors — with the benefit of GPS devices and satellite downlinks — now place it. Much of Thompson's subsequent surveying was even more accurate. Some modern surveyors with a love of history have used period-piece surveying equipment to reenact Thompson's navigational measurements. Even when they can choose good weather days to take their shots, they often find that Thompson's work outshines their own.

Turnor was impressed. In his annual letter to the HBC governors, the astronomer lauded his pupil.

> *I have inserted some observations which were made and worked by Your Honors' unfortunate apprentice, David Thompson. I am fully convinced they are genuine, and should he ever recover his strength far enough*

to be capable of undertaking expeditions I think Your Honors may rely on his reports of the situation of any place he may visit.

But tragedy continued to dog Thompson. As a consequence of his wholesale pursuit of surveying, over the course of one winter he destroyed the sight in his right eye, "by the attention to my calculations in the night, with no other light than a small candle." (One surveyor/historian has speculated that Thompson went blind in one eye, not both, because he observed the altitude of the sun without protecting the eye he used to read the sextant.) Thus afflicted and still lame, Turnor considered Thompson a liability for a surveying trip to the Athabasca Country. Instead, the 19-year-old Thompson was dispatched downstream in the summer of 1790 to transport a load of furs to his old haunt at York Factory. In making the trip, Thompson completed his first field survey, that of the 1200 kilometre-long Hayes River route to Hudson Bay.

To modern readers, the run-together surveying entries in Thompson's notebooks, coded with abbreviations, atypical spellings, odd capitalizations, and inconsistent punctuation, can be confusing.

April 21st [1808]. A fine frosty Morn. Gummed the Canoe & at 6 A.M. set off, Co[urse] N75E $^{1}/_{10}$*S5E* $^{1}/_{10}$*S25E* $^{1}/_{7}$*N35E*$^{1}/_{10}$*S80E*$^{1}/_{10}$*S40E*$^{1}/_{2}$*the beg[ining] of Co[urse] the Rivulet or Brook from the right 8 to 10 Y[ards] wide …*

But the information was reproducible. Thompson later transcribed the twists and turns into points to be plotted onto rough maps, which he forwarded to the HBC governors with his annual letters. The HBC turned this information over to the London cartography company of Aaron Arrowsmith, which produced the maps that became crucial to the exploration of the continent. A century later, some of Thompson's surveys were still the most current available. Thompson never received credit from Arrowsmith for his contributions.

Many have traced the paths of Thompson's journeys. Geologist and historian J.B. Tyrell recreated many on foot, on horseback, and by canoe in the late 1800s, when the ruins of the fur trade posts were still evident. As a result of Thompson's surveying accuracy and attention to detail, and the re-creation efforts of surveyor/historians, only a few questions remain as to locations reached by David Thompson in all of his travels.

Blind in his right eye and with a permanent limp, David Thompson must have made a curious spectacle as he travelled the fur trade routes. Years later, the Salish and Ktunaxa (kah-TOO-na-ha), bemused by Thompson's surveying, named him *Koo-Koo-Sint* — "The Man Who Looks at Stars." Thompson told them and his companions that his sky-watching, "was to determine the distance and direction from the place I observed to other places." Perhaps with a shrug he added, "but neither the Canadians nor the Indians believed me." So, without celebration of his efforts, David Thompson set about his lifework, filling his precious notebooks with crammed column after crammed column of observations and computations, charting every step along the rise and fall of trail, and every twist of rapid and slack water — chipping away at the enormous blanks on the map in an unknown land.

Chapter 3
Crossing the Floor

That the HBC prized the services of its young clerk was obvious when it responded to a request of his in 1790. David Thompson's initial contract was due to expire in May the following year. The standard reward for someone of Thompson's rank who completed his service was a new suit of clothes. In his letter to the HBC governors that autumn, Thompson requested that the price of the clothes instead be put towards a complement of surveying equipment, with extra costs incurred to be levied against his future earnings. When the supply ship returned in the autumn of 1791, Thompson received a new suit, the gift of a brass navigating sextant, and a contract for three years with a raise to £15 per year. The following summer, a gift of more surveying equipment arrived, along with a glowing letter from the governors of the HBC.

Thompson spent the years 1791–96 in the country north of Lake Winnipeg, a land that he referred to with some disdain as the Muskrat Country. Despite the depletion of furs, competition remained intense. The various posts that Thompson and his supervisor, Malcolm Ross, constructed were often but a stone's throw from NWC outposts. Complicating matters, there had been a split within the HBC, which saw the traders at Churchill no longer answering directly to the governors in London. As a result, Thompson, who was still based at York Factory, often competed with factions of his own company as well as with NWC traders.

It was clear to Thompson and to many of his colleagues that the HBC had to expand trade into the Athabasca Country — the Mackenzie River basin of today's northern Alberta, northeastern B.C., and the Northwest Territories. Independent traders, lead by Peter Pond, had worked near Lake Athabasca in the winter of 1778–79. Pond's first haul of pelts was so great, he had to leave half of it behind. Not only were the fur-bearing animals numerous, but the cold climate and the deep forests of the "near north" produced luxurious pelts. But the HBC would not commit to the expansion.

In the summer of 1793, Thompson requested another raise for his next contract. The HBC governors responded by quadrupling his salary to £60 per year — more than his supervisor made — and by presenting him with the gift of a fine pocket watch, itself worth £12. Although he accepted the gift, Thompson silently chafed at the manner in which the HBC dragged its heels.

The trader was now in his mid-twenties. The rugged country in which he travelled began to leave its mark on him. J.J. Bigbsy, who worked with David Thompson in 1817, after Thompson had left the fur trade, provided the only known portrayal of the man.

> *He was plainly dressed, quiet and observant. His figure was short and compact, and his black hair was worn long all [a]round, and cut square, as if by one stroke of the shears, just above the eyebrows. His complexion was of the gardener's ruddy brown, while the expression of deeply furrowed features was friendly and intelligent, but his cut-short nose gave him an odd look.*

In the summer of 1796, Thompson finally received permission to explore a route from Duck Portage, west of Lake Winnipeg, to Lake Athabasca. It was an ill-starred journey. Thompson and his two Chipewyan companions reached their destination but the route was poor. Disaster struck on the return.

> *About half way up the black river, we came to one of the falls, with a strong rapid above and below it, we had a carrying place [portage] of 200 yards, we then attempted the strong current above the [water]fall, they [the two Chipewyans] were to track the canoe up by a*

line, walking on shore, while I steered it ... the canoe took a sheer across the current, to prevent the canoe upsetting, I waved my hand to them to let go the line and leave me to my fate, which they obeyed. I sprang to the bow of the canoe took out my clasp knife, cut the line from the canoe and put the knife in my pocket, by this time I was on the head of the fall, all I could do was to place the canoe to go down bow foremost, in an instant the canoe was precipitated down the fall (twelve feet), and buried under the waves, I was struck out of the canoe, and when I arose among the waves, the canoe came on and buried me beneath it, to raise myself I struck my feet against the rough bottom and came up close to the canoe which I grasped, and being now on shoal [shallow] water, I was able to conduct the canoe to shore.

After the Native guides collected some of the gear — including Thompson's surveying equipment and his records of the journey to that point — they patched the hull with pine gum. On the ensuing journey, with Thompson battered and shoeless, the trio resorted to eating gulls, baby eagles, and swans. They tore the tent into three pieces to use as sleeping blankets. Survival was only assured when they encountered a Chipewyan camp. The Native people provided broth for the wretched men, and in an ironic twist, gave Thompson a kettle, ammunition, and a pair of shoes on credit, with the account to be settled when the Chipewyan next came to trade.

At the conclusion of the trip, Thompson heard from the HBC governors of their wish that he replace Malcolm Ross, who was due to retire the following spring. The imminent promotion apparently did not appease Thompson's frustration at having been kept so long on the dreary turf of the Muskrat Country. He left no written record of his growing discontent, which is surprising, because he spent his last winter with the HBC at Bedford House on Reindeer Lake, an outpost a later trader would describe as, "the most miserable hovel that imagination can conceive." Instead, disregarding the custom and courtesy of providing a year's advance notice of his resignation — required so that the notice could be delivered to England in the autumn and a replacement dispatched on the supply vessel the next spring — on May 22, 1797, Thompson informed Malcolm Ross that with his "time being out," he intended that day to quit the HBC for the rival NWC. His notebook entry was equally succinct.

> *This day left the service of the Hudson's Bay Co. and entered that of the Company of Merchants from Canada [NWC]. May God Almighty prosper me.*

As if to underscore his resolve, Thompson set off from Reindeer Lake at 3:30 the next morning in a snowstorm to make the 140-kilometre journey by snowshoe to the nearest NWC outpost. It is difficult to imagine Thompson "defecting" in such circumstances unless he was certain to secure employment with the NWC. No surviving evidence supports the assumption that he had struck a deal with his new employers in advance, but as slighted as the HBC felt to see Thompson go, the NWC was equally as exuberant to receive him.

Chapter 4 The Man of the Moment

The beginning of David Thompson's service with the NWC coincided with a significant change in the relationship between Britain and the U.S. At the end of the American Revolution in 1783, Britain and the nascent U.S. agreed to establish a border between their unsettled territories in North America. This was accomplished by the Jay Treaty of 1794, which specified that the border would run through the centres of Lake Superior, Rainy Lake, and Lake of the Woods, from where it would follow the 49th parallel west to an unspecified point. The country beyond was largely unknown at the time, and France claimed much of it as "The Louisiana Territory."

Sentiment in the U.S. was building to restrict British

trade in the unsettled territory south of the 49th parallel. Wise to this economic patriotism, the NWC realized that it needed to know the precise locations of its farthest-flung outposts and trading areas, to prevent itself from remaining committed to assets that might soon fall under U.S. control. David Thompson, with his demonstrated surveying skills, was the man of the moment. As the HBC was reeling from Thompson's defection, the senior partners of the NWC ushered the surveyor to their annual meeting at Grand Portage on Lake Superior, where he received his first assignment and a raise that doubled his salary.

Writing some 50 years later in his *Narrative,* Thompson summarized his mission for the NWC, and gloated while sniping at his former employer.

> *Wherever I could mark the line of the 49th parallel of latitude [I was told] to do so, especially on the Red River. Also, if possible to extend my surveys to the Missisourie [Missouri] River; visit the villages of the ancient agricultural Natives who dwelt there; enquire for fossil bones of large animals, and any monuments, if any, that might throw light on the ancient state of the unknown countries I had to travel over and examine. The Agents and Partners all agreed to give orders to all their trading posts, to send men with me, and every necessary I required [was] to be at my order. How very different the liberal and public spirit of this North West Company of Merchants of Canada; from the mean selfish*

policy of the Hudson's Bay Company styled honorable; and whom, at little expense, might have had the northern part of this continent surveyed to the Pacific Ocean …

Thompson left Grand Portage on August 9, 1797. Travelling with a fur trade brigade, he followed the standard route west, across Rainy Lake and Lake of the Woods, and down the Winnipeg River to Lake Winnipeg. Separating from the brigade, he made a circuit of trading houses in what is now Manitoba, taking fixes of their positions. After drawing a cursory map, which he forwarded to the agents of the NWC, Thompson and a party of nine "free traders" struck off from a trading post near the confluence of the Souris and Assiniboine rivers, to trek across the Great Plains to the villages of the Mandan. They left at an unlikely time — late November — and soon paid for the lapse in judgment. On the second day, the temperature was –29°C; by the fourth day it had fallen to –38°C and a gale was blowing. Relief came on the sixth day with a temperature of –18°C, which Thompson characterized as "mild."

After 33 days, during which time they narrowly avoided an ambush by Sioux warriors, Thompson's party arrived at the cluster of Mandan villages on the Missouri River in what is now North Dakota. The surveyor recorded the life of these people in incredible detail, differentiating between the customs of the individual villages, including a vocabulary of 375 words and recognizing three tribes: Mandan, Hidatsa, and

Arikara, (groupings with which modern anthropologists agree). Thompson described how the Mandans used hoes fashioned from the shoulder blades of bison and deer to cultivate crops of corn, pumpkins, beans, and melons. He remained with the Mandans for two weeks, but could not entice them to travel north to trade as they were afraid of the Sioux.

After returning from the Mandan villages Thompson spent three weeks transcribing his field notes and preparing for another leg of his assignment. On this outing, he intended to find the source of the Mississippi River, suspected to be close to the 49th parallel. Under the terms of Jay's Treaty, any land west of the Mississippi River and north of the 49th parallel would remain open to Canadian trade. The NWC operated several trading houses in the area of question.

Thompson proposed travelling by dogsled but his men were reluctant. They suspected what Thompson could not imagine — that spring would be upon them before the journey was complete. The surveyor had spent the previous winter — among the coldest ever recorded in Canada — on Reindeer Lake, nine degrees of latitude north of where he now proposed to explore. His men were right. By late March, the hapless party faced unnerving travel on the fragile ice of rivers and streams. Taking to the riverbanks, they slogged in the rain in knee-deep snowmelt, carrying on their backs what supplies had to remain dry while the dogs dragged the floating sleds. The party was soon caught outright in the spring breakup. They ran for their lives across disintegrating river ice to the refuge of a trading outpost.

By early April the flood subsided and Thompson and his men had crafted a six-metre birchbark canoe, the first of many he would construct on-the-spot to facilitate his explorations. Travel upstream from the outpost was difficult, in a country that he described as, "something like an immense swamp." They were in the wild-rice wetlands of what is now northern Minnesota.

The river ice thickened as they progressed south and gained altitude. Undeterred, Thompson directed his party to build a sled, onto which they loaded the canoe and the baggage. Alternately dragging the sled and paddling the canoe in an arduous 19-day journey from the outpost, they travelled the 90 kilometres to Turtle Lake, just south of the 48th parallel, which Thompson proclaimed to be the northern source of the Mississippi River.

In 1832, the American explorer and naturalist, Henry Rowe Schoolcraft, deemed Itasca Lake — some 50 kilometres distant from today's Big Turtle Lake — to be the river's source. Most present-day references concur, but not all contemporary hydrologists agree. Some insist that, as the Missouri River is a tributary of the Mississippi, the source of the Mississippi River lies at the headwaters of the Missouri River in Montana. But consult any American reference on the matter and you probably will not find any mention of David Thompson, who preceded Schoolcraft to the vicinity by

34 years, when the land was known only to the Native peoples and a handful of NWC traders.

Not yet tired, Thompson hitched a canoe ride from Turtle Lake with a party of Chipewyans. After turning north up a tributary of the Mississippi, the paddlers crossed a height of land to the southwestern shore of Lake Superior. At this point in his *Narrative*, Thompson inserted a calculation of the elevation of Turtle Lake, which he gave as 450 metres above sea level, along with the comment that, "all the public can expect, or obtain, [in the way of measurements] in these almost unknown countries, are the estimates of experienced men." The lake known today as Big Turtle Lake is at a mean elevation of 410 metres above sea level.

The surveyor was just a short-hop by canoe from Grand Portage. However, he took a characteristically Thompsonian route to the NWC's western head office, making a counter-clockwise circuit of the world's largest freshwater lake in order to plot the locations of NWC posts along its south shore. It was typical for Thompson to have fortuitous meetings in unexpected places. His arrival at Sault Ste. Marie coincided with that of the NWC's principal agents, Alexander Mackenzie and William McGillivray, who were bound from Montréal to the annual meeting of the partners at Grand Portage. After summarizing his journey for Mackenzie, the senior trader remarked that Thompson had, "performed more in two months than he expected could be done in two years." Ten days later, Thompson hitched another ride, this one to Grand Portage in Mackenzie's canoe. He did not have to lift a paddle but he did continue his survey, completing the first chart of the shoreline of Lake Superior.

As a result of Thompson's epic winter journeys of 1797–98 — in which he covered 6440 kilometres — the NWC saw that it had to abandon many lesser posts. More importantly, it needed to relocate its western hub from Grand Portage, which was in U.S. territory. This, the company accomplished in 1803, when Fort Kaministiquia (later called Fort William) opened for business at the present site of Thunder Bay. Although used seasonally, the NWC's new clubhouse in the wilds was the largest habitation that far west on the continent. Almost a thousand workers had laboured in its construction. A spiked palisade ringed the fort, which encompassed 42 buildings (including a boatyard, and a cooper's shop for making barrels) on its 125 acres. The NWC ran a small farm nearby to supply fresh food. Inside the palisade, agents and partners dined like kings and princes, while outside, paddle-weary hordes of voyageurs drank, caroused, and squabbled away the time between their journeys on the brigades.

Chapter 5
Frozen Smoke and a Madness of Mosquitoes

Ninety years before the Canadian Pacific Railway and nation building became Canadian obsessions, the NWC established the first trans-continental transportation system in North America. NWC traders routinely moved people, goods, and furs along an intricate network of rivers, lakes, and portages, to outposts as distant as 6400 kilometres from Montréal.

At the centre of this remarkable enterprise was an unlikely union — the brawn of proud, human sinew, riding within fragile shells of birchbark. The voyageurs (French for "travellers") supplied the muscle. This corps of paddlers hailed principally from what was then Lower Canada — today's province of Québec. They applied their collective strength to a simple yet effective technology inherited from the Algonquin — the birchbark canoe. The Algonquin used bark from the yellow or white birches that grew in the mixed forests of eastern Canada. They wrapped the bark around a lightweight cedar frame, and, using awls of bone, stitched the individual bark pieces together with thin spruce roots called "watape." The canoe builders coated the seams with spruce gum. The resulting craft, brilliant in its simplicity, opened almost an entire continent to travel.

Two pulses of NWC brigades plied the continent's waterways each year: those heading west carried new employees, supplies, trade goods, and written instructions; those heading east carried the year's take of furs, letters, and the requisitions for supplies and trade goods. The brigades met near the head of Lake Superior in mid-summer, where cargoes and stories were swapped.

After paddling at a pace of 45 strokes per minute for 14 hours each day, sleep came easily to the wracked bodies of the voyageurs. But none could seek his blanket until the canoes were checked for damage and all the seams were re-gummed. At daybreak, the voyageurs reloaded the canoes. The brigades bound from Montréal to Grand Portage packed almost two tons of supplies into each vessel. When possible, the voyageurs rested for five minutes each hour — in a sheltered bay on a lake, or in slack water on a river — during which time they stoked their pipes. They came to measure a section of a journey by the number of "pipe breaks," which equated to the number of hours travelled. In a "good pipe" they covered 12 kilometres.

Celebrated for their paddling prowess, the voyageurs demonstrated at least half their worth on the portages. A portage — unloading a canoe and carrying it and all of its gear — was necessary when the current was too swift to paddle against, or when rapids were too dangerous to run. A portage could be a few hundred metres around a single waterfall, but many were longer. The Grand Rapids portage, where the Saskatchewan River emptied into Lake Winnipeg, was five kilometres long. According to David Thompson, it required, "two or three days labor." The Grand Portage, (French for "Great Carrying Place"), at the head of Lake Superior, was named for its 13.7-kilometre length. The Methye Portage into the Athabasca River system was 20 kilometres long.

No matter what the load — be it trading goods, voyageur food or pelts — the NWC packed the freight into 90-pound "pieces." Each voyageur was responsible for eight pieces. On a portage, he would hoist a piece to his back, securing it by means of a leather tumpline around his forehead. With the load in place, a fellow paddler would heave another 90-pound piece into place, nesting it atop the first. Thus loaded, the voyageur would jog to the next put-in place. The voyageurs broke the longer portages into 800-metre sections. At the end of each, they dropped their loads before returning for more. If he carried two of his pieces at a time, a voyageur would traverse each way along the length of a portage four times. In this fashion, the Grand Portage became a 110-kilometre epic, requiring a week. Some of the voyageurs would pack three or four pieces on each leg, earning a cash reward. There is an account of one voyageur repeatedly carrying five pieces, or 450 pounds, throughout the day.

A voyageur's work was already the definition of toil, but two aspects — bugs and winter — put the job description over the top. The thawing masses of ice and snow, the travel in open canoes through Shield country, the muskeg of the Hudson Bay lowlands, and, eventually, the thick forests of what is now B.C. — this was a recipe for hell in bug heaven. No fur trader who kept a journal failed to devote page space to bugs. David Thompson's mentor, Philip Turnor, recorded this account.

> *Upon this carrying place [portage] the musketoes [mosquitoes] are intirely mad, the two men that went over the carrying place first had their legs, thighs, hands & face intirely covered with them and no sign of their skins was to be seen ...*

Thompson first became acquainted with biting bugs at the HBC's forts on Hudson Bay.

> *Summer, such as it is, comes at once, and with myriads of tormenting musketoes; the air is thick with them,*

there is no cessation day nor night of suffering from them … The narrow windows were so crowded with them, they trod each other to death in such numbers, we had to sweep them out twice a day; a chance cold northeast gale of wind was a grateful relief, and [we] were thankful for the cold weather that put an end to our sufferings.

He may have been thankful for cold weather in summer, but not in winter.

We builded log huts in which to pass the winter, the chimneys were of mud and coarse grass, but somehow did not carry off the smoke, and the huts were wretched with smoke, so that however bad the weather, we were glad to leave the huts …

On the 18th of December at 8 A.M. the thermometer was –56; at noon –44; and at 9 P.M. 48 degrees [Fahrenheit] *below zero. It was a day of most intense cold, the ice on the lake was splitting in all directions, the smoke from the chimneys fell in lumps to the ground.*

Beyond his early years with the HBC, David Thompson was not often at the paddle and rarely packed portage loads, but he nonetheless endured the extremes of the seasons for 28 years, which makes his accomplishments as a surveyor all the more remarkable.

Chapter 6
Bright with the Beams of the Sun

After his first assignment for the NWC, David Thompson took six weeks of rest at Grand Portage before embarking on a rambling two-year journey that took him in and out of the Athabasca Country. It was there that he met and married Charlotte Small, aged 14, who was half Scottish and half Cree. The notebook entry for their wedding day was detailed, but in a Thompsonian way. "The event took place on June 10, 1799 at Lat. 55.26.15 N, Long. 107.46.40 W."

Thompson was perhaps the first Canadian worker for whom there is a record of a corporate "bait and switch." He was initially lauded with the title, "official geographer and explorer of the NWC," and was permitted to look for fossils on company time. But within a year, Thompson's sole duties mirrored that of a clerk. In this capacity, he assisted various wintering partners with the commerce of the fur trade.

In 1800, Thompson's travels brought him and Charlotte to Rocky Mountain House, near the present-day Alberta community of the same name, at the confluence of the Clearwater and the North Saskatchewan rivers. The HBC ran a shop called Acton House at the same location. Both companies intended these outposts to become stepping stones in the first trade forays across the Rocky Mountains, where furs were rumoured to be numerous, and the Native peoples willing to trade.

Thompson's instruction was to await senior NWC partner, Duncan McGillivray, whom he would accompany in an attempt to cross the Rockies. In their plan, Thompson and McGillivray confronted more than unknown geography. One of the major obstacles to crossing the mountains would be the simmering hostility between two First Nations: the Piikani (pee-CAN-ee) who lived on the eastern slopes of the mountains, and the Ktunaxa (kah-TOO-na-ha) who lived to the west. The Piikani, armed with muskets obtained in the fur trade, had driven off the traditionally-armed Ktunaxa, and had gained control of the mountain passes. Although they were willing to act as middlemen in trade with the Ktunaxa, the Piikani did not want to lose their advantage by having the fur traders move west. One of the tactics used by the Piikani was to portray the Ktunaxa as dangerous. Most traders saw through the ploy but it nonetheless had something of the desired effect. With their constant hassling, the Piikani engendered a sense of anxiety that effectively undermined the fur trade, and which ultimately, for David Thompson, would cause a crisis at a crucial time.

McGillivray was late in reaching Rocky Mountain House, so Thompson, having heard that some Ktunaxa were on their way to trade, formed a party to go out and meet them. Their route took them southwest to the Red Deer River, which they followed upstream. At the present-day site of Sundre, Thompson recorded — 13 years after his first view of the Rockies — his second impression of the mountains.

> *Here we had a grand view of the Rocky Mountains, forming a concave segment of a circle ... All its snowy cliffs to the southward were bright with the beams of the sun, while the most northern were darkened by a tempest ... which spent its force only on the summits.*

Even as late as 1800, perhaps only a few dozen Europeans — beginning with HBC trader Anthony Henday in 1754 — had seen the Rockies. To the early white explorers, the Rockies existed in mythical form, the sweep and the extent of the mountains constructed in their minds from secondhand accounts and from maps scratched in the dirt by Native peoples. The general impression was of a single range of mountains which, once crossed, would provide access to the Pacific Ocean. Any explorer who might make that crossing would be the first to complete a useful northwest passage by land, and would be guaranteed a place in history.

As they travelled south along the Red Deer River into the mountains, Piikani warriors fell in with Thompson's party. The trader noted another hazard of the country — "grisled [grizzly] bears but too many." Near the headwaters of the river, Thompson met the Ktunaxa trading party. After smoking the customary pipe of greeting, the trader and the Ktunaxa camped.

The next day, a Piikani raiding party descended and attempted to steal a Ktunaxa horse. The Ktunaxa leader, whom Thompson called Old Chief, was fed up — the Piikani had been pilfering horses for the duration of their easterly trek. Thompson and one of his voyageurs spent the evening pleading with Old Chief to continue on. He agreed. But after dark, the Piikani stole five more horses. Thompson was able to escort the reluctant Ktunaxa to Rocky Mountain House, but the Piikani continued their raids and harassment. By the time the Ktunaxa were ready to depart the fur trade fort they had no horses. Thompson gave one of his horses to Old Chief, and sent two traders, Charles La Gassé and Pierre Le Blanc, to accompany him for the winter. It is often said that this pair became the first white men known to have crossed the Rockies — the southern Rockies, perhaps, because Alexander Mackenzie had crossed the northern Rockies in 1793.

A few hours after the departure of La Gassé and Le Blanc, Duncan McGillivray arrived. Anxious to see the mountains that Thompson then described to him, McGillivray hastened to make a trip to the south, deep into Piikani territory. The NWC had a plan to bring Native trappers to the Plains, because the Piikani expressed no interest in trapping furs. But first, McGillivray wanted to visit the Piikani winter camps along the Highwood River, to see what the chiefs thought of the idea.

The two traders and four companions left Rocky Mountain House on horseback on the unlikely date of November 17. They covered the 270 kilometres to the Piikani territory, southwest of present-day Calgary, in six days. At the two Piikani camps that the traders visited, the chiefs agreed to the NWC plan to import others to trap furs, while lamenting the fact that their enemies across the mountains, the Ktunaxa and the Salish, were now armed as a result of the fur trade. To this, Thompson replied, "that they themselves, the Pekenows [Piikani], had first and principally armed the Kootanaes [Ktunaxa] in exchange for horses & c [etc.]." This was true, but fell short of admitting the source of the muskets obtained by the Piikani — the NWC and the HBC.

After spending six days hunting bison and deer, McGillivray turned the party west along the Bow River toward the Rockies. They stopped near the present site of Exshaw, where McGillivray, Thompson, and one of the men — no doubt prodded by Thompson's desire to see the lay of the land — ascended a mountain. Here, as he often did when describing the mountains, Thompson became poetic.

Our view from the heights and eastward was vast &

unbounded — the eye had not strength to discriminate its termination: to the westward hills & rocks rose to our view covered with snow, here rising, there subsiding, but their tops nearly of an equal height every where. Never before did I behold so just, so perfect a resemblance to the waves of the ocean in the wintry storm.

It is not clear which peak Thompson's party ascended. But to this trio goes the credit of making one of the earlier recorded ascents of any mountain in Canada. Thompson's description of the rocks they encountered is typical of the limestone of the area: "When the rock was solid, it was extremely rough and full of small sharp points like an enormous rasp — this enabled us to mount places very steep, as the footing was good & sure, but it cut our shoes, socks &c [etc.] all to pieces in a trice." Their shoeless condition in early December might explain the speed of their return to Rocky Mountain House. They were home in three days.

Duncan McGillivray had brought west with him transcriptions from Captain George Vancouver's *Voyage of Discovery to the North Pacific Ocean*, which, among other things, chronicled Vancouver's exploration of the mouth of the Columbia River in 1792. As he wintered at Rocky Mountain House, David Thompson studied that text and copied passages into one of his own notebooks, preparing himself with the best available information to use after he crossed the mountains.

When Old Chief had departed Rocky Mountain House

A 1957 five-cent postage stamp featuring David Thompson
(© Canada Post Corporation, reproduced with permission
from the National Archives of Canada, POS-000424)

in the autumn of 1800, he had promised to send a guide the following spring to lead Thompson west. This he did, but the guide, who came back accompanied by La Gassé and Le Blanc, was murdered by Stoney men not far from the outpost. In replacing that guide, Thompson and McGillivray made an inexplicable choice. Instead of selecting La Gassé or Le Blanc, they quickly rounded up a replacement named The Rook, who claimed to have crossed the mountains before. The Rook was a Cree whom Thompson described as "timorous" and "wavering" and "addicted to flattering & lying." The Rook so ably served the purpose of thwarting success that he might well have been in league with the Piikani.

On the proposed departure date, Duncan McGillivray was ill. He assigned James Hughes, the man in charge at Rocky Mountain House, to take command, with Thompson to assist. The party left Rocky Mountain House on horseback on June 6, 1801. In an exasperating week-long journey, The Rook first led them along the North Saskatchewan River, encountering steep banks where horses fell and gear disappeared. After a harrowing ford of the river to its south bank, the party thrashed along the North Ram River — sometimes in mud so deep as to brush the horses' bellies — to a snow-filled, dead-end at its headwaters. The difficulties for once vanquished the poet in David Thompson.

> *The scene around us has nothing of the agreeable in it, all nature seems to frown, the mountains are dreary, rude & wild, beyond the power of the pencil.*

When his irate charges finally cornered The Rook to account for his incompetence, the guide replied that on his previous crossing of the mountains by this route, "we had no horses with us — we left them with our families, at the entrance into the mountains ... I forgot [about] this part of the mountain[s]: you see plainly as well as me that if we go farther, we must leave our baggage & horses."

After a tentative probe on foot, Hughes and Thompson conceded defeat. When they got back to the North Saskatchewan River, Hughes took the horses and the hopeless guide and returned to Rocky Mountain House. Thompson and eight men constructed a canoe and made an attempt to paddle *up* the North Saskatchewan River. But the snowmelt was at its peak. Paddling against the current was impossible. The men poled and lined the canoe, and sometimes resorted to pulling the boat upstream by grabbing at trees along the riverbank. Thompson finally abandoned the plan. Taking to the swollen river in the canoe, the men shot the 120 kilometres to Rocky Mountain House in less than six hours, "paddling no more than what was necessary to keep the current from carrying us on the rocks or against the craigs [crags] of the river." This was "Little Ice Age" snowmelt, perhaps triple or quadruple the typical volume of late spring today.

At the outpost, Thompson met his first child for the first time. Fanny had been born on June 10, the second anniversary of his and Charlotte's marriage. His absence at the births of his children would be a recurring theme. Five of the couple's 13 children were born while he was employed with the NWC, but he was not present a single time. His notebooks and his *Narrative* are largely silent on his family. But it is likely that Charlotte's life, trundling along rough trails, bumping along in canoes, and wintering in damp, smoky outposts — with babes in tow — was the epitome of hardship.

The cloud of failure occasioned by The Rook's incompetence yielded a silver lining.

Whoever wishes to attempt to cross the mountains

for the purposes of commerce ought to employ a canoe, & start early in the spring, say the beginning of May … In this season, they would cross a great part of the mountains without extraordinary difficulty, and meet the flushes of high water where they have need of it, that is, near the head of the river — from whence there is said to be a short road [trail] to the waters which flow on the other side of the mountain[s].

Thompson had described the plan well, but matters of commerce soon intervened. The HBC and a new enterprise, the XY Company — headed by former NWC partner, Alexander Mackenzie — were trading into the Athabasca Country. Thompson's superiors closed Rocky Mountain House and dispatched him north in the spring of 1802. Away from the mountains, he spent the next four-and-a-half years trading and trapping, while on the side he took shots of the stars, and nurtured his dream of reaching the Pacific Ocean.

Chapter 7
Upstream to the Ocean

When David Thompson returned to Rocky Mountain House in October 1806, he was a partner in the NWC, having been given two shares. The XY Company and the NWC had merged and the HBC had all but given up on the Athabasca Country. A new threat to trade had materialized, and to Thompson's joy, it forced the NWC to focus again on finding a route across the Rockies.

In 1803, France sold to the U.S. the Louisiana Territory — lands south of the 49th parallel between the Mississippi River and the Rocky Mountains. In typical American fashion, President Thomas Jefferson wasted no time in exploring the new area. The expedition of Meriwether Lewis and William

Clark marched west along the Missouri River in May the following year, ironically aided by a map of the Mandan country produced from David Thompson's survey of 1797.

Lewis and Clark were not content to stop at the mountains. In November 1805, they pulled up at the mouth of the Columbia River, where they wintered in a cluster of cabins named Fort Clatsop. On the return journey in July 1806, Lewis and Clark separated to more fully explore the country. Along the Two Medicine River in what is now Montana, Lewis scrapped with the Piikani peoples, killing two. Word of the killings spread quickly among the First Nations, charging the atmosphere of the fur trade.

Lewis and Clark had established a tentative American presence west of the Rockies, but it was in an area where boundaries were not settled and where trade was virtually untapped. With its established network of outposts leading to the eastern foot of the mountains, the NWC possessed a clear advantage. The company hurriedly put into place a plan to compete with the Americans. It would be a push on two fronts, rooted in the existence of a mythical river.

The quest for a Northwest Passage from Europe to the Orient endured as the central theme of global exploration, from the first voyage of Columbus in 1492, to the epic undertakings of Franklin in the 19th century. In 1778, Captain James Cook mapped the west coast of North America, in the process somehow missing the mouths of the Columbia and Fraser rivers. Along the Alaska panhandle Cook described an opening that became known as "Cook's River." The Captain speculated that the river could be used as, "a very extensive inland communication." The theory was bunk. Captain George Vancouver visited "Cook's River" in 1794 and found it to be the bay now known as Cook's Inlet. But in the interval between Cook's planting of the seed and Vancouver's assessment of the opening, a myth germinated that would promote the exploration of western North America.

The first to take up the quest to approach the Pacific Ocean from the headwaters of Cook's imaginary river was the independent fur trader, Peter Pond. In 1785, he drew a map of the Athabasca Country that showed "Cook's River" flowing from the west shore of Great Slave Lake to the Pacific Ocean. Pond canvassed the British and U.S. governments, as well as the NWC for support to mount an expedition along the river, but nothing came of it. He quit the fur trade in 1788. A year later, the fledgling NWC gave Alexander Mackenzie, a young trader who had wintered with Pond in the Athabasca Country, the assignment of descending "Cook's River" to the Pacific Ocean.

Mackenzie made two epic attempts — journeys pivotal in Canadian history. In 1789 he followed the river that now bears his name, but disappointingly to the pack ice of the Arctic Ocean. Four years later he traversed a system of rivers and portages south and west from the Peace River in what is now Alberta, intending to descend a river he called "Tacoutche Tesse" — now known as the Fraser River. When rapids on the upper Fraser deterred him, he struck off overland, stringing together rivers, marshes, and mountainsides in a heroic trek to Dean Channel on the Pacific Ocean. There, using a paint made of vermilion and bear fat, he left a brief inscription on a rock, the ultimate understatement: "Alex Mackenzie, from Canada by land, 22[n]d July 1793."

In his second journey Mackenzie had, in a fashion, pioneered the long sought Northwest Passage. But it was a useless route for the fur trade. What the NWC required was not more portaging, but a navigable river with a good port at its mouth, from which to ship furs around Cape Horn to Montréal. Just such a river seemed to materialize when word of the exploits of Captain Robert Gray reached the east. In May 1792, Gray had anchored his vessel, *Columbia Rediva,* at the mouth of a large river near the 46th parallel. Gray named the river after his boat, and claimed the river and the surrounding territory for the U.S. Captain George Vancouver visited the river that autumn, and dispatched a rowboat and crew across the bar at its mouth and a good distance upstream. Vancouver claimed the river for Great Britain.

Returning from his journey to the Pacific Ocean in 1793, Mackenzie learned of Gray's and Vancouver's explorations. He became convinced that the upper reaches of the river that he had descended in 1793 (the Fraser River), were the headwaters of Gray's and Vancouver's Columbia River. Mackenzie pitched a plan to the NWC to explore the river but, despite the support of Duncan McGillivray and others, the plan fizzled. Mackenzie quit the NWC in disgust and founded the XY Company.

More than a decade later, the NWC finally resolved to push trade west to the Pacific. The company gave its partner, Simon Fraser, the assignment of establishing a series of trading outposts in what is now northeastern B.C. In 1808, from one of these posts, Fort George (now the site of Prince George), Fraser descended the river now named for him. Fraser characterized the route in a telling journal entry, four weeks into the trip. "I have been for a long period among the Rocky Mountains, but have never seen anything equal to this country, for I cannot find words to describe our situation at times. We had to pass where no human being should venture."

When he reached tidewater, Fraser did not look upon an open reach of ocean that matched the descriptions of the mouth of the Columbia River in Gray's and Vancouver's journals, but into the Straits of Georgia. Mackenzie had been wrong; the Fraser and the Columbia rivers were not the same. Confronted with this failure and with harassment by Native peoples, Fraser made his retreat.

The NWC charged David Thompson with the other half of its push to the Pacific. When Thompson arrived at Rocky Mountain House in the autumn of 1806, the way had been prepared. Earlier that summer, a Métis trader named Jaco Finlay had cut a trail to the headwaters of the North Saskatchewan River, and down the Pacific slopes into

Ktunaxa territory. When Finlay returned in November, he drew a map of the route for Thompson.

Ktunaxa trading parties came to the fort several times that winter and into the spring of 1807, when in April they reported that the depth of snow on the Pass through the Rockies was still, "equal in height to the top of a tall Pine." Thompson waited. He and his men built dog sleds with which they moved and cached supplies upstream to lighten the loads for the springtime canoes.

The party left Rocky Mountain House on May 10, 1807. Although the North Saskatchewan River was low, its waters were swift and frigid. The surveyor lead a string of packhorses along the riverbank and noted that the paddlers were, "continually wet up to the waist" in water, "so excessively cold as to deprive them of all feeling in their limbs."

Thompson was travelling with a cumbersome entourage that included Charlotte and their three children, a family of one of the voyageurs, and the wife of another. His horse string met the canoe party at Kootenay Plains, a prairie in the front ranges of the Rockies. There he left the canoe, the families, and the horses in order to proceed upstream on foot with the voyageurs.

Two days later they reached the vicinity known today as Saskatchewan River Crossing, where the North Saskatchewan River makes a sharp northward bend to its headwaters at the Columbia Icefield. There it also receives two principal tributaries — the Mistaya River from the south, and the Howse River from the southwest. Thompson and his men advanced a short distance along the Howse River to camp. The way ahead was still snow-choked, so Thompson and one voyageur, a man named Bercier, remained with the supplies while the others returned to Kootenay Plains. Three days later, Thompson and Bercier made the first recorded visit to Glacier Lake. Although tempted by the abundant tracks of moose, the pair could kill nothing. It was the beginning of a harvest of hunger.

For almost two weeks Thompson waited for the snow to melt, while the voyageurs brought the trading supplies and food upstream from Kootenay Plains. He passed the time making boxes in which to pack the gear for the upcoming horse trip. Finally, on June 22, the trader could bear the frustration no longer. He and Bercier rode two horses the 19 kilometres to the "Portage of the Mountains," now known as Howse Pass, in just over three hours. Taking note of the first westward flowing stream, Thompson commented, "may God in his mercy give us to see where it's waters flow into the ocean & return in safety." The pair descended 10 kilometres on the Pacific slope, studying the steepness and the canyons of what is now known as the Blaeberry River. They were back at camp after an absence of just 12 hours. Thompson dispatched Bercier next day with instructions for the entire outfit to join him for the crossing of the mountains.

They assembled on June 24 but the new arrivals, "brought not a mouthful of provisions." Next day the party set off for Howse Pass. The horses were in poor condition and Thompson, out of necessity, held up the proceedings while he went hunting mountain goats. It was an outing from which he nearly failed to return.

> *I found the mountain, altho' apparently not above an [angle] of 45°, almost too steep to climb: when I breathed a few seconds, I was obliged to keep hold with my [finger]nails & feet to prevent myself sliding down — at the same time keeping fast hold of my gun, which otherwise would soon have found [its way to] the foot of the mountain in pieces.*

Thus delayed, the party made it only to a, "little marshy meadow full of springs" on Howse Pass on the night of June 25. With the horses weak and the party still short of food, they carried on, descending the Blaeberry River along, "a very woody bad road." Thompson let go a blast at trailblazer, Jaco Finlay.

> *From what has been said of the road of the portage [the trail across Howse Pass], it is clearly seen that Jaco Finlay with the men engaged last summer to clear the portage road, has done a mere nothing ... Jaco ought to lose at least half his wages for having so much neglected the duty for which he was is expressly engaged ...*

The words carried weight. By the time the next trading season arrived Jaco Finlay was finished as a NWC trader. He and Thompson met frequently over the next two years, and although their relationship might initially have been cool,

Finlay freely assisted Thompson, often feeding him and his men. Later, he would work for Thompson again.

Five days after crossing Howse Pass, Thompson's party pulled up on the bank of the Columbia River where Finlay had built and stashed canoes the previous summer. Perhaps because he had learned of the river from the Ktunaxa (whom he called "Kootanaes"), Thompson called it the "Kootanae River." What happened next has baffled some historians, but is easily explained by Thompson's intent and by his needs of the moment — chiefly food. After building a canoe, the trader turned his party *upstream* on the Columbia, hoping to find the Ktunaxa on their home turf and get some grub.

Philip Turnor, the HBC surveyor from whom Thompson had learned his craft, had proposed a simple method for finding the Pacific Ocean — follow any major river downstream on the west slope of the Rockies. This was the technique that Alexander Mackenzie attempted to use in 1793, and that Simon Fraser employed successfully in 1808. Some have labelled Thompson's ascent of the Columbia River a "wrong turn," but where Thompson first met the river, it flows north, not west, and would not have been an obvious choice for a route to the Pacific Ocean.

Thompson's route brought more worries than lingering concerns about the Piikani. It took almost two weeks for the party to construct a large river canoe to accompany the two smaller ones left by Finlay, and for the men to backtrack and bring the remaining goods down from where they had been cached on the descent from Howse Pass. During this time, one of the voyageurs almost died from the sufferings of a pain in his flank. In time, a porcupine quill worked its way through his skin. Thompson speculated that the man, "had in eating the meat [of a dog] swallowed the porcupine quill in the meat, as he is a voracious eater." By this time, there were no dogs left to eat. The party was saved from starvation when some Ktunaxa hunters provided deer meat.

On July 12, the canoes were ready and loaded. While a voyageur named Broulard and a few Native people lead the string of horses along the river, Thompson joined the others in paddling upstream, lamenting that, "as I am obliged to paddle I cannot take the courses of the river, but refer it to some other more convenient opportunity."

Alternately dipping at the paddles and attempting to hunt and fish, the party struggled upstream for a week, south to Lake Windermere, near present-day Invermere. In one journal entry Thompson recorded that they, "hunted and fished but all of us without success — a partridge [grouse] among all of us for supper." Slim pickings for 17 people. Thompson derided Broulard, who arrived a few days later with only three of the brigade's 24 horses. While searching for a building site, Thompson and his men found the body of a wild horse that Ktunaxa hunters had killed the day before. Desperate for food, they took some of it back to camp and boiled it. Everyone ate a piece and soon all were violently ill.

Thompson needed to establish an outpost from which

to ship furs east that autumn. On July 19, his men began a crude building on a terrace above the lake. Without horses to aid in hauling logs, the labour of staying put was at least equal to that of moving.

> *The men were now so weak, that however willing, they actually had not strength to work, & some of them told me that two or three days more of famine would bring them to the ground.*

The famine endured, and yet they carried on. Thompson tallied each day's food intake in his notebook: a single fish, a few pounds of pemmican traded from the Ktunaxa, another solitary grouse, nothing in 300 metres of gill nets. In a letter to his supervisors, the trader wrote about the predicament that dogged him from sunrise each day until, "sleep at last relieves me from a train of anxious thoughts."

On the advice of a visiting Ktunaxa man, Thompson reconsidered the location of the outpost and, in a move that must have been tremendously unpopular with his men, decided that the building was too far from water and not defendable. He abandoned the partly completed fort and chose another site downstream, near the confluence of Toby Creek and the Columbia River. Here Thompson and his men set about building Kootanae House, which when completed three months later, became the first NWC outpost west of the Rockies.

As the NWC men were building the outpost, a band of

Piikani arrived, saying that they were pleased to see the traders, but Thompson thought otherwise. He called them, "professed dissimulators" and stated that, "they have it in their power to be very troublesome to us." The Ktunaxa who had been camped nearby, and who had been trading sporadically with Thompson, apparently felt the same, for they soon moved inside the confines of the partly completed outpost, placing themselves under the protection of the fur traders. With a laconic comment in his notebook, Thompson ably described his remarkable ability to keep the peace: "It is fortunate that I am not off on discovery." According to Thompson, the Piikani war chief was still Kootanae Appee. Perhaps remembering his promise to protect the trader, made at their meeting in the spring of 1788, the chief chose to spare Thompson and his men.

Thompson's luck with food improved at the end of August when the chinook salmon run reached Lake Windermere. His men took to spearing fish by torchlight, and soon became proficient. But the fish, although as large as 34 $^1/_2$ pounds, were in poor condition, being near the end of their spawning journey. Despite the cautions of the Ktunaxa, the fur traders threw the salmon carcasses to their dogs. Thompson summarized the effect: "For about 6 days past our dogs have been dying, & this day made their exit." With the contingent of dogs wiped out, there was one less species of critter on the menu. The occasional deer, duck, swan, or trout rounded out the scanty food of the traders.

In the fourth week of September, Thompson dispatched an eastbound brigade by canoe to deliver the season's meagre take of furs across Howse Pass, and to return with the trading supplies for the next year. A few days later, the Old Chief of the Ktunaxa, whom Thompson had dealt with in 1800, arrived at Kootanae House in the company of Ugly Head, a Salish chief, so named because of his unruly hair. From Ugly Head, Thompson learned about the river along which the Salish lived. After plying him with much tobacco, Thompson persuaded Ugly Head to guide him there.

They left on horseback on October 2. Within the day, they had passed along the shore of Columbia Lake, now recognized as the source of the Columbia River. At the south end of the lake, the party crossed what Thompson called "McGillivray's Portage," the unremarkable height of land, now known as Canal Flats, that just barely separates the Columbia River from the Kootenay River. The Kootenay River he called "McGillivray's River." The names commemorated his colleague, Duncan McGillivray, who would die the following year without ever hearing of the tributes.

The party forded the Kootenay River and carried on a short distance to where Thompson became aware of a misunderstanding. It had been his intent to follow the river as far as it was navigable. Ugly Head now wanted to head overland to deliver Thompson much more quickly to the river's mouth. They resolved the misunderstanding, although communication was difficult. Thompson first had to translate his intent from English. Then, "what I say in French is to be spoken in Blackfoot, then in Kootanae, then in Flat Head [Salish] etc. etc. so that the sense is fairly translated away before it arrives at the person [being] spoken to."

Bidding farewell to Ugly Head, Thompson and his party retraced their steps to Kootanae House. They found nothing amiss, but his people were, "under apprehensions of an attack" by the Piikani. News came to the traders of war between the Piikani and the Salish — who lived in present-day Montana and Idaho — where 14 Piikani and four Salish had been killed. To the Salish, this was a tremendous victory. To the Piikani it served notice: their dominance of the west slope tribes was over.

The tension endured all winter. Thompson thwarted an outright assault by the gift of a pipe and tobacco, delivered by Ktunaxa messengers to Kootanae Appee. The war chief, not wanting to risk losses attacking a building, "that a [musket] ball cannot go through, and with people we cannot see and with whom we are at peace," accepted the gift and took his warriors back over the mountains, leaving the traders to their business.

Thompson spent the spring of 1808 exploring along the Kootenay River. Although he had arranged to meet some Ktunaxa guides, the rendezvous did not take place. The NWC traders were left to tackle the unknown route by themselves. Near where today's Kootenay River crosses the U.S. border, they entered a grassland where the Ktunaxa had told him they grew tobacco. Thompson called it Tobacco Meadows — today's Tobacco Plains.

The party made a harrowing portage along the cliff edge above Kootenai Falls, after which they nearly came to grief in the rapids downstream. Their diet was never sufficient. It included skunk and a cougar, and a rotten deer carcass, which made them violently ill. In a letter to the senior partners of the NWC, Thompson penned an understatement: "I labour under many disadvantages which only time and a generous assistance can overcome." Another notebook entry reads: "Went fasting to bed." And another: "Here we made a meal of a few berries." But as an indication of their resourcefulness, the surveyor and his men had requisitioned crop seeds for the trip. The first sowing at Tobacco Plains was barley, peas, and turnips. In later years, Thompson and his men experimented there and elsewhere with potatoes, corn, rice, and beans.

After three weeks, the hungry men reached Kootenay Lake. The Ktunaxa First Nation had two cultures. The "upper" culture dwelled near the mountains, and crossed them to trade and to hunt bison. The "lower" culture was centred at Kootenay Lake. Thompson alternately called the lower culture, the Lake Indians or Flat Bows (rhymes with "cows"). He commented on the unusual design of their canoes — known as "sturgeon-nosed" — in which the bow and the stern curved forwards and backwards, respectively, to the waterline. The only other area where this canoe design is common is in Siberia.

From the Lake Indians, Thompson learned that Kootenay Lake emptied into a river that combined with a much larger river about 80 kilometres downstream. But they told him that it was no easy journey. The initial reach involved five portages around a chain of waterfalls — one of which required a day and a half. Thompson was torn between his desire to see if the route offered passage to the Columbia River, his obligation to establish trade, and his need to return to Kootanae House to prepare the eastbound shipment of furs. Given the difficulties of the journey to that point, he gave in to the needs of commerce, and backtracked to where the Kootenay River entered the lake. But in the few days that he had been absent, the Kootenay River and its tributaries had flooded, preventing further travel to make contact with the local Native peoples, and blocking them from coming to him to trade.

It was time to head home. Thompson hired Old Chief to guide his party back to Columbia Lake — a difficult journey that required 12 days. Thompson's take on the foray to Kootenay Lake was just three bales — less than 300 furs. His men lost one of the bales when, after trying unsuccessfully to cross the Moyie River on a logjam, they lined the goods across and the line broke.

Reaching Kootanae House, Thompson barely gave himself time to catch his breath. The eastbound brigade had left with the winter's furs. These included 100 goatskins, which eventually sold in London for a guinea each — more than twice the value of the finest winter beaver pelt. Orders were taken for more goatskins at half that price again. The NWC instructed Thompson to hunt goats, and mocked him the following year when he replied that goat hunting was too dangerous and too time consuming. To reward their "ignorant ridicule," Thompson told the partners that he would send no more goatskins, and kept his word.

The eastbound brigade included children and women, among them Charlotte, who was pregnant with their fourth child. Taking to the Columbia River in a light canoe, Thompson soon caught up with them. On the climb along the Blaeberry River to Howse Pass, the trader recorded two events that underscored the perils confronted by his family when they accompanied "dad" into the mountains.

> *One of my horses nearly crushing my children to death with his load being badly put on, which I mistook for being vicious, I shot him on the spot and rescued my little ones.*

At least the mishap provided some food. Thompson and his men butchered the horse and packed its flesh for rations. On the next day, tragedy nearly struck again.

> *At 3 P.M. we reloaded [the horses], but missing my little daughter [probably two-year-old Emma], and nowhere finding her, we concluded she was drowned & all of us set about finding her — we searched all the embarrass [logjams] in the river but to no purpose. At length Mr. McDonald found her track going upwards. We*

searched all about & at length thank God at 8 1/2 P.M. found her about 1 mile off, against a bank of snow.

Apparently, it took brushes with death for Thompson's children to receive mention in the scant page space of his precious notebooks.

The remainder of the journey was relatively event-free, with only the regular hassles and dangers. Snow had crushed the canoe that Thompson's men had "put-up" on the east side of Howse Pass the previous autumn. So the trader bartered with Iroquois trappers for a replacement. In their new craft, the brigade took to the North Saskatchewan River, paddling only to prevent collisions with rocks. The women (as did probably the men) paled as the canoe swept through the whitewater, propelled by a winter's worth of snowmelt. The current was so fast, and the paddling so dicey, Thompson did not attempt to plot the river's course.

After feasting on fresh bison at Kootenay Plains — their first meal of sound meat in more than a year — the brigade reached Rocky Mountain House on June 25. They had been gone 13 months. Jaco Finlay, working now as a free trader thanks to Thompson's rebuke, was camped nearby. Whatever sentiments may have lingered, neither deferred from commerce. Thompson traded with Finlay for a solid haul of furs.

A day's paddle downstream, Thompson dropped his family at the outpost called Boggy Hall. His brigade carried on at an astonishing pace to the new NWC western depot at Rainy Lake, just east of today's Manitoba-Ontario border. The

NWC had moved its depot west from Fort William because some wintering brigades were now travelling so far west and north, they could not make the trip to meet the eastern brigades and return to their outposts in a single season.

Thompson arrived at Rainy Lake on August 2, unloaded his furs, packed a load of trading goods, and departed on August 4. On his return to Kootanae House, he stopped at Boggy Hall just long enough to welcome his new son, John, born in his absence. Leaving Charlotte and the children there for the winter, Thompson's brigade crossed Howse Pass, troubled by fresh snow and by frozen canoes. After following a small herd of bison down the Blaeberry valley, they took to the Columbia River, arriving at Kootanae House on November 10. In their absence of 156 days they had travelled 4800 kilometres.

Chapter 8
The Dance of Discovery

David Thompson's best guess was that the Columbia River would deliver him to the Pacific Ocean. But first he had to find the needle of the river's current in the haystack of valleys west of the Rocky Mountains. His exploration played out as an unhurried dance of discovery, choreographed by opposing interests. The magnet of the unknown drew him west — first to the mountains, then across them — while his obligation to commerce held him in place or pulled him east. The path that resulted was like a transverse spiral extending westward, on whose looping course he repeatedly moved two steps closer to, then one back, from his ultimate objective.

In his insatiable desire to learn about the land,

Thompson accumulated knowledge from every possible source. Wherever he stopped to trade he would query the Native peoples, seeking to discover how the valleys connected, finding out if the next reach of river was navigable, asking them whether they had ever been to the "Great River," as the Columbia was known. Time and again the Native peoples drew maps in the dirt with sticks or with their fingers. In this manner Thompson claimed a profound knowledge of the landscape, enabling him to depict with great accuracy areas where he had not travelled. His map of 1814 shows seven tributaries of the Bow River in the vicinity of present-day Banff National Park, and gives names to five of them, although in his own travels Thompson only ever saw two of those tributaries. His ability to accurately fill blanks on the map with secondhand information was nothing short of magical.

But in many cases, Thompson's mapping was based on firsthand observation, and the more familiar he was with a place, the more detailed was his map. He travelled the reach of the Columbia River between Kootanae House and the mouth of the Blaeberry River six times. His map painstakingly records the myriad twists and turns of the wetlands there. In other cases, he mapped using the inference of firsthand observation, as when he ascended a ridge along the Pend Oreille River in 1809. Off in the distance he could see the valley of the Columbia, if not the river itself. Thwarted on that trip and on a subsequent attempt to descend the Pend

Oreille River, his map records the intervening reach of water as "Unnavigable."

By cleverly balancing his commitments to commerce and his desire for discovery, Thompson began to understand how a river that flowed north for hundreds of kilometres from its source at the 50th parallel, flowed west into the Pacific Ocean at the 46th parallel. As he wintered at Kootanae House late in 1808, he must have considered the possibility that the river just outside the door — a river he called the Kootanae River — was in fact the Columbia River.

Thompson had many seasons of accomplishment, but his greatest as a trader was in 1809. In June he travelled east from Kootanae House with the brigade, but stopped off at Fort Augustus (near present-day Edmonton). There he probably heard of Simon Fraser's descent of the Fraser River, with its implication: the Columbia was a different river. He was back at Kootanae House in mid-August, from where he departed south over familiar ground to commence his real work of the year, the exploration of what he called the "Saleesh River" — today's Flathead, Clark Fork, and Pend Oreille rivers.

As Thompson and his clerk, Finan McDonald, moved south, they checked the Tobacco Plains garden. The peas had not germinated, the turnips were worm-eaten, and only a few stalks of barley showed promise. After a chance meeting with some Ktunaxa who helped them portage Kootenai Falls, the pair engaged some Salish peoples and their horses, and struck south from the Kootenay River, overland to Pend

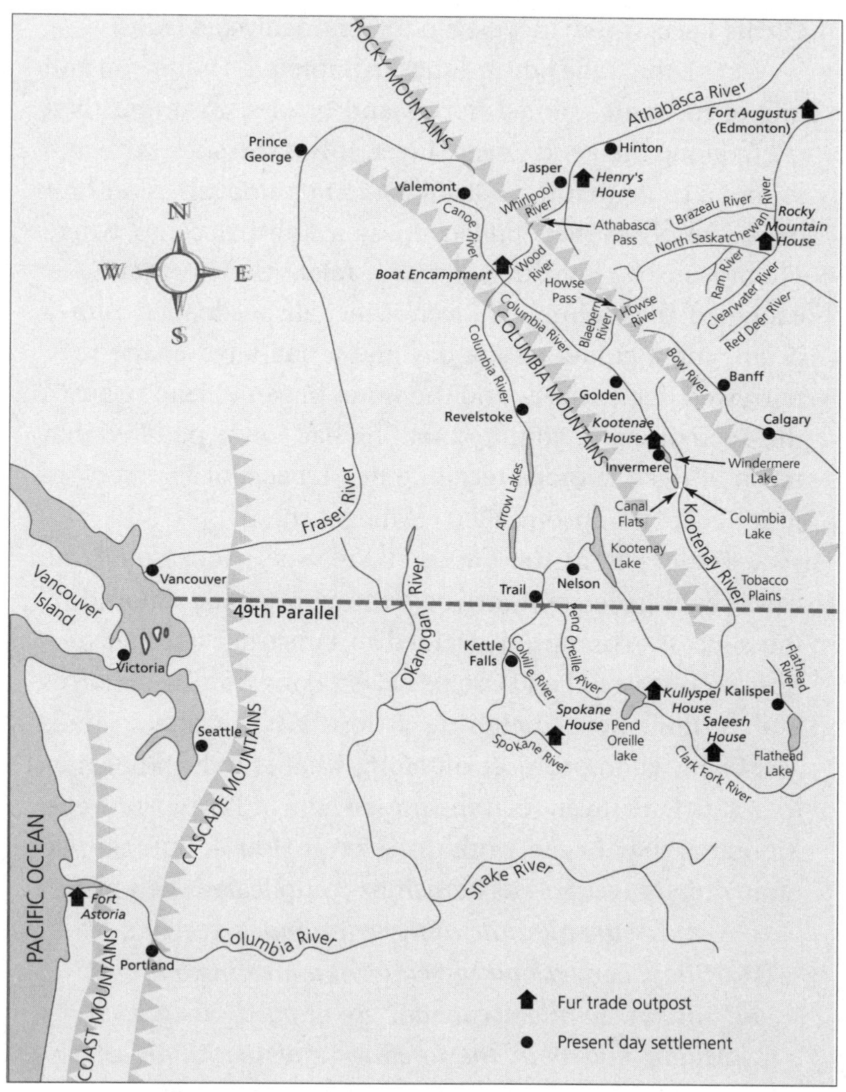

Exploration of the Columbia River; 1807–1812

Oreille Lake, where they began to build Kullyspel House.

With the trade house almost completed, Thompson and one of his men saddled horses and headed west and then north along the Pend Oreille River. It was the surveyor's aim to find a route that the Piikani could not ambush. After four days, the NWC men pulled up at a Kalispel camp where Thompson was told that it was a relatively short jaunt by canoe to the Columbia River. The Kalispel loaned him a canoe and a guide, who, a day and a half later, as the river narrowed dangerously, and the water began to leap beneath the decrepit craft, admitted that he had never paddled that reach of river. Perhaps recalling the debacle of The Rook in June 1801, Thompson called off the journey.

Trade was in full swing at Kullyspel House, and the westerly brigade soon arrived with more goods. Buoyed by the success, Thompson decided to construct another outpost, southeast of Pend Oreille Lake. Taking a string of horses and a few men, including fellow NWC trader, James McMillan, Thompson set off along what is today known as the Clark Fork River. Near the present site of Thompson Falls, Montana, they began work on Saleesh House. But, as it so often did, hunger and its hardships complicated their plans.

> *As we are all quite hungry and much in want, Mr. McMillan, Forcier and myself went a hunting but without success. By the accidental going off of his gun Mr. McMillan had both the forefingers of his hands shot through by ball & much lacerated with the powder, both*

of his fingers are broke & seemingly will with difficulty be kept from falling off — I dressed them as best I could.

But it was not enough. The finger had, "a bad appearance and no hopes of joining with the stump [so] I separated it." The matter of hunger was neatly solved by the appearance of Jaco Finlay and his family, who traded beaver tails and dried meat. The free trader's opportune arrival may have at last softened Thompson's impression. He soon rehired Finlay as clerk and interpreter.

By great fortune, Thompson had located Saleesh House on a major travel route for the Salish, Kalispel, and Ktunaxa. Besides trading for furs, he could trade for food, so the preoccupation with hunger sank into the background. Free traders working the area, glad to have a depot so close, frequented the house. The furs piled up.

In late February, Thompson and one of his men headed southeast to the Flathead Valley, where they learned from the Ktunaxa and Salish that the Piikani had killed a lone American trader nearby. Thompson saw enough to verify the story. This reminder of the Piikani's vengeance cast a grim shadow over his successes.

Returning to Kullyspel House, he dispatched Jaco Finlay overland to the southwest to construct Spokane House on what is today known as the Spokane River. Thompson bought a canoe — one of only two times he recorded doing so — and hired a Kalispel guide to take another crack at following the Pend Oreille River to the Columbia. The 30-metre drop of

Metaline Falls brought them up short, some 50 kilometres from their destination. The guide advised Thompson that a dangerous portage requiring two and a half days lay ahead. An alternate overland route would eat up even more time — time that Thompson did not have. The easterly brigade was due to depart. But being so close, Thompson could not simply turn his back on the great river of the west. He scampered up a hill for a better look.

> *I now conceived the Columbia River was in a deep valley at the north end of these rude hills ... Alternately surveying the country, and considering the information I had collected from the various Indians, I concluded that we must abandon all thoughts of a passage this way, and return by our old road [the Howse Pass trail], till some future opportunity shall point out a more eligible road.*

From this passage in his *Narrative*, it would seem that David Thompson, when he next returned west, intended to cross Howse Pass and *descend* the Columbia River. It was a sensible plan, but for once, the tricks that would thwart it would not be those of topography.

Chapter 9
We Now Bend Our Course

David Thompson's life of exploration shone with many accomplishments, but dark clouds of controversy mark the year 1810. The man who kept meticulous notebooks that detailed his daily movements and activities for almost 24 of his years in the fur trade, left no record for three pivotal months that year. In his *Narrative*, written some 40 years later, Thompson briefly described a few events, but assigned only one date (incorrectly) within that time. His account is contradicted by the journal of NWC trader, Alexander Henry the Younger. The discrepancies are so great that some historians have accused Thompson of destroying a notebook and of subsequently lying in his *Narrative*. The most incriminating detail is

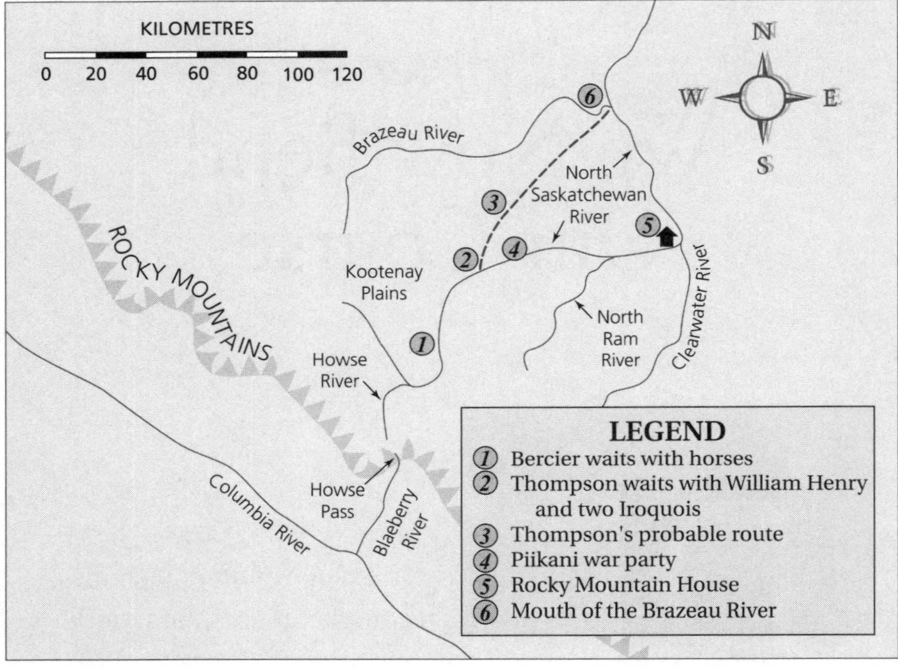

The North Saskatchewan River and the Canadian Rockies

that Thompson's notebook entries recommenced immediately after the events in question, and with no mention of those events.

The spring season of 1810 began routinely enough, with Thompson joining the eastbound brigade, destined for a leave from duty. The NWC wisely gave wintering partners a year off every so often, to prevent them from becoming "bushed." It is likely that when Thompson left Kootanae

House in early June, he was bound for Montréal, where he and his family could have expected to arrive by mid-August, and to remain until the following April. For some reason, the family's plans changed. Charlotte and their three youngest children stopped at Winnipeg House with her sister-in-law. (The couple's oldest daughter, Fanny, then ten, had been at boarding school in Montréal for a few years.)

Thompson carried on, but a messenger cut short his eastward trek at Rainy Lake on July 22. Carrying orders from the senior partners at Fort William, the courier directed Thompson to return to the Columbia Department — as the NWC called the new trading area west of the Rockies — to look out for the company's interests in the face of the expected arrival of John Jacob Astor's, Pacific Fur Company. Astor and the NWC had entered into an agreement earlier in the year. The two companies would share trade along the Columbia River, with the NWC receiving one third of the furs. The American trader was preparing his vessel, the *Tonquin*, to sail from New York around Cape Horn to the mouth of the Columbia River.

Tensions were high between Britain and the U.S. The NWC had unsuccessfully petitioned Britain to provide naval security at the mouth of the Columbia River. In the absence of big guns and government interest, the company saw that traders in canoes would have to fly the flag and keep an eye on the prospects for commerce. Thompson knew all this when he made his U-turn in the lake country of the Canadian

Shield, but because the lag in communication between Montréal and the western outposts was so great, neither Thompson nor anyone else in the west knew that the deal between Astor and the NWC had fallen through soon after it had been proposed.

It has become a Canadian legend that in 1810–11, David Thompson "raced" the Americans to the Pacific Ocean. Some historians have criticized the trader for "dallying" in all his exploration west of the Rockies, "wasting" four years (1807–1810) at the end of which, the Americans, in the form of the Pacific Fur Company, "beat" him to the mouth of the Columbia River by a few months. In "losing the race," some historians have further faulted Thompson, pointing out that his delay cost Britain a good chunk of empire — its claim to the Oregon Territory.

The legend and those arguments, while a good story, are unfounded. When David Thompson first crossed the Rockies in 1807, it was with a two-fold aim of plotting an effective trade route to the Pacific Ocean, and of establishing commerce along the way. Although it required four years, his efforts, with their many comings and goings across the mountains, were successful on both counts. In his final push to the Pacific in 1810-11, Thompson was not in a great hurry. He had three active fur trade posts in the Columbia Department — Saleesh House, Kullyspel House, and Spokane House — all of which, as best he knew, were doing great business. He thought that the NWC and the Americans were in a partnership, and he knew that it was unlikely that the *Tonquin* had yet made it to the mouth of the Columbia River. If there was any race in the summer of 1810, it would have been between the NWC and the HBC. While heading east on the North Saskatchewan River in June, Thompson had met two westbound HBC canoes, "well arranged for the Columbia." Joseph Howse, the trader for whom Howse Pass was subsequently named, was in one of them.

What we know about events as David Thompson approached the Rockies in 1810, is largely due to the journal kept by Alexander Henry the Younger. Henry and Thompson were colleagues who had wintered together at outposts in the early 1800s. Relying mostly on Alexander Henry's account, and deferring occasionally to Thompson's *Narrative,* we can sketch the confusing, but dramatic events along the North Saskatchewan River in August, September, and October 1810.

As he neared the mountains, Thompson split his westbound brigade into three. With fellow trader, William Henry (Alexander's cousin), and two Iroquois, Thompson rode into the mountains to hunt, while a second group paddled and lined the canoes up the North Saskatchewan River. Thompson planned to meet this canoe brigade later at the site of Rocky Mountain House, at that time abandoned. Thompson had also sent a trader named Bercier farther ahead with horses to use in crossing Howse Pass. Bercier waited for the others with the horses, upstream at Kootenay Plains.

Thompson, for reasons we will never know, chose not to follow the North Saskatchewan River into the mountains, but — perhaps pursuing animals on the hunt — headed into the woods. His route cut off a great bend in the river, which he reached about 80 kilometres west of Rocky Mountain House, near the present-day community of Nordegg. Thompson had travelled the North Saskatchewan valley enough to know where he was. He decided to wait for the canoes, using the time to dry the elk meat from the hunt. One of the Iroquois Thompson was with announced a portentous dream, saying, "this meat will never be eaten," as he walked out of the camp and out of the story.

Meanwhile, Thompson sent William Henry and the Iroquois downstream to find the second group — his canoe brigade. The pair soon came upon four tents of a Piikani war party. The Piikani First Nation was outraged at its defeat by the Salish in a skirmish near Saleesh House the previous winter. Seven warriors died — two probably killed by Thompson's man, Finan McDonald, who had been alone at the outpost. The war party was not going to permit traders to cross the mountains at Howse Pass.

William Henry and the Iroquois fired a "warning shot" and returned, without finding the canoe brigade. When informed of the news, Thompson berated the men and made a quick plan for departure. He sent the one remaining Iroquois to Kootenay Plains with a message for Bercier, instructing him to lead the horses downstream to the mouth of the Brazeau River. There, Thompson and William Henry would wait. In all this confusion, what is not clear is how or where Thompson planned to find the missing canoe brigade. He must have known that they would be past the mouth of Brazeau River by the time he got there.

If this were the sole version of events, historians might have left David Thompson alone. But in his *Narrative*, Thompson sabotaged himself by concocting an elaborate story. First he stated that William Henry and the Iroquois, when they first went downstream to look for the canoes, found where the canoe brigade had defended itself against an attack at a place where, "there was blood on the stones." After William Henry and the Iroquois rejoined him, Thompson reported that the three of them stayed together as they were pursued by the Piikani, thwarting capture only when a snowstorm covered their tracks and a trio of grizzly bears deterred their pursuers. Thompson admitted to an absence from his men of two days, when the truth was that he was missing for more than three weeks. He also stated that he rode directly to Rocky Mountain House after the encounter with the Piikani.

William Henry's cousin, Alexander Henry the Younger, intended to reopen Rocky Mountain House that autumn. Travelling in advance of his own men, he met up with Thompson's canoe brigade at the outpost. Alexander Henry took charge and attempted to sort things out for the voyageurs, who were wondering where their boss was. A group of Piikani descended upon the trading post. In anger, they disinterred two Cree buried in the cemetery and scattered their bones. They also opened the grave of a fur trader's daughter. Perhaps realizing that they had overstepped the bounds of decency, they left the coffin alone. No matter, wolves soon ripped it and the corpse apart.

This rattled both Alexander Henry and Thompson's canoe brigade. Thinking that Thompson was still upstream on the North Saskatchewan River, Henry hurried Thompson's brigade off in that direction. A Piikani chief soon arrived and told Henry that no canoes would be allowed to pass upriver. The chief caught up with the canoes the next day. The voyageurs, aware that any misstep could set off the Piikani, attempted to convince the chief that they did not wish to cross the mountains, but merely to winter in the area. The chief, wise to the ploy, replied that if that was the case, the fur traders may as well winter downstream at the fur trade post. The voyageurs blinked. Two days later, they pulled up for the second time at Rocky Mountain House.

The Piikani war party from the original blockade soon arrived at the outpost. In their possession, they had David Thompson's horse and a pair of leggings that belonged to William Henry. Alexander Henry did not let on his concern, but deduced that Thompson must still be upstream on the North Saskatchewan River. The comings and goings of the Piikani, and the reluctance of the voyageurs to travel under the threat of reprisal, thwarted attempts to dispatch the canoes to find him. Finally, Alexander Henry resorted to trickery. He sent the voyageurs with the canoes downstream during the day, instructing them to return upstream in the dark, by which time he expected to have all the Native people roaring drunk and oblivious. The plan worked. But the next day, to Alexander Henry's astonishment, his cousin William Henry arrived from *downriver*, with Alexander Henry's own canoe brigade, saying that David Thompson was waiting for his men some 80 kilometres downstream, at the mouth of the Brazeau River.

Because David Thompson left us no day-by-day record, many have interpreted from these events. The most uncharitable scenario is that Thompson lost his nerve. For 24 years, he had been conducting difficult travels in wild country, with meagre equipment and supplies. Time and again he had proven himself an innovator, always equal to whatever hardships the elements, his men, the Native peoples, or the senior partners of the fur trade had pitched to him. For 10 of those years, he had contended with the extra layer of danger engendered by the uneasy relationship between the white fur traders and the Piikani. As Thompson had seen for himself along the Flathead River in the spring of 1810, the Piikani were ambushing and killing lone fur traders. Since long before that, the Piikani and their Nitsitapi allies had been razing fur trade outposts. Who wouldn't have cracked under the strain, and later destroyed a notebook to conceal the evidence?

An equally likely scenario is that Thompson, if not outright lost, was at least disoriented. As he was travelling by horseback, his surveying equipment was probably in one of the canoes. (The fact that he popped out on the North Saskatchewan River far to the west of his intended destination, Rocky Mountain House, suggests that he was disoriented.) In backtracking to try and find the canoe brigade, he would not have followed the riverbank trail, where the Piikani would have easily discovered him. He and William Henry plunged into the black spruce thickets and the dense forest of the Rocky Mountain foothills. Thompson may have been attempting to duplicate the route he had just followed into the mountains, but he could not have expected the 130-kilometre journey to take the better part of two weeks. But such are the forests of the Rocky Mountain Foothills because apparently, it did.

Three questions remain. Did Thompson lose a notebook during this perilous time? Or, would the embarrassment of being disoriented have been cause for him to destroy a notebook rather than to rip out a few incriminating pages? Or, was he not keeping a notebook because he was not taking compass shots and sextant readings?

After William Henry finally arrived at Rocky Mountain House, Alexander Henry hopped into one of his newly arrived brigade's canoes and headed downstream to the mouth of the Brazeau River, where he found Thompson. Henry reported that, "this affair of his canoes being stopped by the Peagans [Piikani] has induced him [Thompson] to alter his route and endeavour to open a new road [trail] from North branch [the Brazeau River] by Buffalo Dung lake to Athabasca river, and thence across the mountains to the Columbia ..."

Alexander Henry tried to talk Thompson out of the plan, pointing out that the Piikani war party had, at least temporarily, removed its blockade on the North Saskatchewan River. He suggested that Thompson could make a quick dash across Howse Pass. But Thompson may have been aware of the personal threat to him now posed by the Piikani, and certainly did not wish to face future encounters with them in the twice-yearly crossings of Howse Pass. So he opted for a more northerly route, out of the Piikani's grasp, "for which place we now bend our course."

Alexander Henry crossed Howse Pass by dogsled in January of 1811, thwarting the Piikani again by first heading downstream and then doubling back. This was the last recorded crossing of that pass until 1859. David Thompson was again blazing a trail and, soon, everyone trading in the Columbia Department would follow.

Chapter 10
The River Revealed

As if it hadn't missed a beat, David Thompson's *Narrative* picks up again on October 29, 1810, after a silence of more than three months. On that day, his regrouped, Columbia-bound brigade, lead by an Iroquois named Thomas, departed along the Stone Indian Road, a rough route that connected the Brazeau and Pembina rivers. Muskeg and windfalls choked the "road." The men spent half of each day cutting passage for the horses.

Thompson was now almost two months behind schedule. In his eagerness, he got underway before all the provisions and men were assembled. On November 1, he sent two men back to Rocky Mountain House with a letter. In his own journal, Alexander Henry the Younger summarized the communication.

> *He [Thompson] was then upon the Panbina [Pembina] River with all his property, on his way to the waters of the Columbia, cutting his road through a wretched thick woody country, over mountains and gloomy maskagues [muskegs] and nearly starving with hunger, animals being very scarce in that quarter ... in fact, their case is pitiful.*

Henry's assessment was partly true; moose abounded in the Pembina country. But the skill of the hunters in the party was only occasionally up to the task. It was Napoleon Bonaparte, a contemporary of Thompson, who stated: "An army travels on its stomach." The saying probably did not yet have currency in Thompson's day, at least not in the wilds of western North America, but the trader already knew its truth. So many of his travels had been plagued by hunger that it would have been sensible for him to prepare better for this monumental journey. He was attempting a new route, with winter coming on, and with the largest group of his career: 21 voyageurs, a few of their wives, a guide, and a hunter. But his notebook entry for the first day set the tone as it concluded: "No supper."

As November dragged on, Thompson's men began to announce their collective displeasure with a primitive form of work-to-rule. They insisted on eating breakfast before packing camp, sometimes wasting the morning. They did not travel as a cohesive group. Some dropped parts of their loads, necessitating frequent backtracking. Thompson often wrote, "hunters nothing" in his notebook entries. It was November 29 before the party, "thank heaven, came upon the Athabasca River." On the way they had experienced two mornings with temperatures of –36°C.

The brigade turned upstream and within a few days was in the teeth of an Athabasca Valley sandstorm, with a south wind scouring the dunes and the river flats at Brulé Lake. Travel on the river ice was treacherous. Thompson was, "thankful that several of the horses are not killed — they have received many and severe falls." When the party halted on December 4, the men began building a depot. Preparations for crossing the mountains consumed the remainder of the month. The men constructed eight sleds for the dog teams, and 13 pairs of snowshoe frames. Native women threaded netting onto the frames. Thompson complained that, "the line [netting] for the snow shoes is very bad, from the awkwardness of the women." No wonder. He recorded the temperature that day as –34°C.

On December 14, Thompson dispatched seven men to Rocky Mountain House to secure food from Alexander Henry. In his journal, Henry recorded that Thompson's men had eaten a horse and five dogs during their 17-day trip. Henry had so little food to give them, it would not have been enough to feed just the seven voyageurs during their return to Thompson. Still looking for a meal, those seven hungry men exited the story, the first of many to abandon the trek.

On December 21, Thompson scratched out a long letter to his friend, Alexander Fraser, at whose outpost he had first stopped when he joined the NWC in 1797. In it, Thompson admitted that the years were taking their toll.

> *I am getting tired of such constant hard journeys; for the last 20 months I have spent only bare[ly] two months under the shelter of a hut, all the rest has been in my tent, and there is little likelihood the next 12 months will be otherwise.*

With arrangements complete, and with fewer men to feed, Thompson's brigade nonetheless had trouble hitting its stride as it made the southward push along the Athabasca River into what is now Jasper National Park. The hunters secured sheep and bison, but the bounty simply promoted gluttony. On January 1, the men ate two large kettles of meat — a kind of frigid brunch (it was –31°C) — that delayed departure until 1 P.M. They travelled 15 kilometres in three and a half hours, then camped again. Thompson exclaimed, "I never saw such an indolent set of men." The sleds were too heavy for the dogs, which Thompson noted, "are very little worth & are much beat[en] by the men."

Thompson decided to hoard supplies. Having seen a food cache farther down the Athabasca Valley destroyed by animals, he left this one in the care of his clerk, William Henry. The precise location of the supply post, subsequently known as Henry's House, is unknown, but it was probably in the vicinity of today's Jasper Park Lodge. The brigade, now numbering 16, moved on. Just before the party turned up the Whirlpool River for the final approach to Athabasca Pass, they left the horses at a place where, "a herd of buffalo [bison] had recently been feeding." This was today's Prairie de la Vache ("Cow Prairie"), near Wabasso Lake.

The conditions that Thompson described along the Whirlpool River would send modern "ski tourers" packing. The temperature swung from –34°C to 0°C. The snowshoes penetrated about a metre, making each step a colossal labour. Thompson broke his pair. The snow balled up under the wooden sled runners and the dogs floundered. A particularly troublesome voyageur by the name of Du Nord, whom Thompson characterized as, "a poor spiritless wretch ... beat a dog senseless — & the sled we made got broke & was with the dog thrown aside."

It was along the lower Whirlpool River that Thompson took note of large animal tracks that had, "4 large toes, ab[ou]t 3 or 4 in[ches] long & a small nail at the end of each; the ball of his foot sank ab[ou]t 3 in[ches] deeper than his toes; the hinder part of his food did not mark well. The whole is ab[ou]t 14 in[ches] long by 8 in[ches] wide & very much resembles a large bear's track ... We were in no humour to follow him: the men and the Indians would have it to be a young mammoth and I held it to be the track of a large old grizled [grizzly] bear ..." Others have suggested that this is the first written description of the track of a Sasquatch — the mythical, ape-like being of the deep forests of western North America.

The Whirlpool Valley approach to Athabasca Pass, even in good conditions, would not have been an easy route in winter. George Simpson, later governor of the HBC, crossed the Pass in 1824, when he wrote, "the track is in many places nearly impassable and it appears extraordinary how any human being should have stumbled on a pass through such a formidable barrier ..."

Dropping bits and pieces of their load as they progressed, Thompson's grumbling party crested Athabasca Pass late in the afternoon of January 11, 1811. In his *Narrative*, the surveyor penned a few lines inspired by the mystery and the remoteness of that place.

> *My men were not at their ease, yet when the night came they admired the brilliancy of the stars, and as one of them said, he thought he could almost touch them with his hand ... Many reflections came on my mind; a new world was in a manner before me ...*

Lofty contemplation aside, the griping of his brigade now tainted the enterprise. In his contingent of voyageurs, Thompson had two breeds: men who had been in the mountains before (some of whom had travelled with Thompson), and those to whom the mountains were new. Du Nord and two others were of the latter stripe, and were given to complaining theatrically about the depth of the snow, the weight of their loads, the steepness of the trail, the choice of route, and a myriad of other matters. Thompson was driven to distraction in dealing with them, yet managed an observation of extraordinary insight.

> *When men arrive in a strange country, fear gathers onto them from every object.*

One of his mens' fears was that they would be avalanched on the Pass. Thompson discounted it, but when he crossed the Pass for the fourth and final time in May 1812, its crest was buried under avalanche debris — "heaps of snow in wild forms, round which we walked."

Thompson was not the first trader to cross Athabasca Pass. The rumour at the time was that a couple of free traders and Native people had been across it a few years earlier. But, for all practical purposes, the route was unknown. It would soon become the mainstay of the western fur trade, and would remain so until trade declined in the 1850s. But as significant as the first crossing of the Pass was to the history and the shaping of Canada, an uncharacteristic surveying blunder was ultimately more important in the local scheme of things.

> *The altitude of this place above the level of the ocean, by the point of boiling water is computed to be eleven thousand feet.*

The altitude of Athabasca Pass is 1750 metres (5742 ft). When botanist David Douglas rambled across the Pass in 1827, he ascended a mountain that he called Mt. Brown. (This was the fourth recorded mountaineering ascent in

Canada.) Eyeballing the difference in elevation between Athabasca Pass and the mountain's summit, he figured that Mt. Brown rose some 6000 feet (1829 m). He added this figure to David Thompson's 11,000 feet (3353 m), and came up with the fantastic elevation of 17,000 feet (5181 m) for Mt. Brown, and also for its neighbour, Mt. Hooker. Perhaps intending to further flatter the senior botanists for whom he named the peaks, he made the preposterous claim that they were the highest mountains in North America. These fictitious giant mountains inspired a cluster of mountaineering expeditions in the late 19th century, journeys that were instrumental in exploring the land that was later included in Banff and Jasper national parks.

As he descended west from the Pass, the mood of Thompson's men dragged him down, so much, that he named the stream along which they travelled, Flat Heart Brook. This is today's Pacific Creek, which flows into the Wood River. While Thompson and a few men plowed their way downhill, others crisscrossed the Pass, ferrying the loads that they had cast aside. In their absence, wolverines had raided some of the untended goods. The monster weasels carried off a five-pound sack of musket balls. More than a century later, a surveyor found 114 rusted musket balls just north of Athabasca Pass, proving that there is at least one thing that wolverines cannot chew.

As paper was in short supply, Thompson wrote a letter on some boards — probably scrounged from packing crates.

William Henry was to transcribe the letter onto paper and forward it to the partners at Fort William. The guide, Thomas, and one of the voyageurs departed as couriers. This reduced the party to 14. Thompson must have considered this a blessing. In a day and a half while they were near the Pass, his crew ate 56 pounds of pemmican, more than one quarter of their supply. Thompson clearly considered this to be gluttony, but the normal ration in the fur trade was two pounds of pemmican, per person, per day. So, travelling in sub-freezing temperatures, the men were a tad hungrier than Thompson had planned, but no hungrier than he should have expected.

As they continued the descent from the Pass, the brigade probably began to wish for cold weather. Rain alternated with snow, drenching the men who were already wet from numerous fords of the Wood River. A later traveller recorded 39 crossings in one day. Attempts to dry gear delayed their departure each morning. Thompson stated that the snow fell like water. It took them nine soggy days to reach the mouth of the Wood River where it emptied into the Columbia River at the Big Bend. Although he knew that the river before him was the Columbia, Thompson, for reasons known only to him, continued to call it the "Kootanae River."

Thompson realized that he could not possibly attempt a descent of the unknown reaches of the Columbia River with his pathetic group of men. So he announced that they would head upstream, some 300 kilometres, to winter at Kootanae House. This triggered a mutiny. As they began their journey south, Du Nord and his cohorts took two and a half hours to travel less than 40 metres. The troublesome trio made their point. Thompson turned the party around to camp for the winter at the mouth of Flat Heart Brook, the prospect of which cleared the ranks. After completing the 40-metre section in a few minutes on their return, Du Nord and his companions deserted. Another booked away ill, and two others Thompson dispatched with more messages for William Henry, from whom they were to return with supplies. Others disappeared, although Thompson did not provide their excuses or their routes.

When the slush settled, Thompson and two companions remained to construct a shelter and to attempt to build a canoe for the spring journey. The birches of the western slopes were small, the bark too thin for canoes. So, after crafting a cedar frame, Thompson and his men laboriously constructed a "clinker built" canoe from cedar boards, stitched together with pine roots. It took them six weeks, during which time they made several starts. Thompson's extensive experience of bending wood for canoe frames, sled runners, and snowshoes must have served him well. The finished product was almost eight metres long and just over one metre wide.

During this time, Thompson hoped that at least some of the men who had deserted would return. But only the two faithful voyageurs dispatched to bring supplies from Henry's House came knocking. The canoe-building project suggested a name for the place: Boat Encampment. Unfortunately, when the Mica Dam was completed in 1973, the location was submerged 160 metres beneath the surface of Kinbasket Reservoir.

On April 17, the party set off upstream. Winter lasted well into spring that year. South on the Columbia River, Kinbasket Lake was still frozen. After waiting in vain for the ice to break, Thompson and his men made a sled and hauled their canoe across the lake. It was May 9 before they found a camping spot not covered in snow. Five days later they reached Columbia Lake.

Thompson was on familiar ground, and he wasted no time. Trading with the Ktunaxa for horses, food, and assistance, his party first travelled to Saleesh House. Because of his skirmish with the Piikani, Finan McDonald had abandoned the post. His whereabouts were unknown. Thompson's men built another canoe with difficulty, and took to the tumult of the Clark Fork River, in flood because of the tremendous snowmelt of that spring. They ran the river to Kullyspel House, which they also found abandoned. Somehow they had missed the outpost's partner, James McMillan, who had already departed east with the winter's furs. Thompson could not leave his trading goods at an abandoned post, so the men were obliged to paddle onwards with the freight, down the Pend Oreille River.

The deserted outposts were an indication of the times and of Thompson's courage. Joseph Howse, the HBC trader whom Thompson had seen heading to the mountains the previous spring, wintered in 1810–11 at an outpost on the Flathead River. One angst-filled season under the watch of the Piikani was enough. Howse pulled out and, on his advice, the HBC abandoned the risky Columbia Department to the NWC.

Hearing from the Native people that Finan McDonald and Jaco Finlay were ensconced at Spokane House, Thompson's party struck off overland for that outpost, which, with the assistance of horses sent ahead to them by McDonald, they reached on June 14. Thompson knew that canoes could not run the precipitous Spokane River below the trading house. As an indication of its former wildness, the 175 kilometre-long reach is today dammed in six places. So he and his men saddled horses for a 100-kilometre ride north over a height of land to the Colville River, which lead the indefatigable explorer at long last to the lower reach of the Columbia River at a place he called Ilthkoyape Falls.

Today, the spot is known as Kettle Falls, although the namesake waterfall lies submerged beneath the reservoir created by the Grand Coulee Dam. "Ilthkoyape" is a Thompsonian derivative of two Salish words: *Ilth-kape*, which means kettle (a cooking vessel woven from roots and cords); and *Hoy-ape*, which means "trap" or "net." Thompson probably meant the basket traps in which the Colville people caught salmon. If so, the name of Kettle Falls is ironic because the completion of the Grand Coulee Dam in 1942, built with wartime haste and without fish ladders, all but killed the chinook salmon run on the Columbia River.

As additional proof that David Thompson was not racing the Americans to the Pacific Ocean, he did not depart immediately downstream. It was two weeks before he had built another cedar canoe and recruited reinforcements for the trip. During this time, Thompson filled his notebook, not with fretting over when he would reach tidewater, but with musings about the life cycle of Pacific salmon.

The brigade took to the river on July 3, 1811 — the only time that Thompson ran *downstream* on a new reach of the Columbia. On his way to the river's mouth, the surveyor stopped at no less than eight native villages, where he took the time for formal ceremonies of greeting, and for chatting up the locals for the purposes of commerce. The Native people often assisted Thompson's brigade with nearby portages. He wasn't racing the Americans, but he did intend to beat them at commerce over the long-term. Near the confluence of the Snake and Columbia rivers, Thompson, noting the lack of a trading house nearby, laid British claim to the surrounding area by writing a notice to that effect and securing it to a pole driven into the ground.

It had taken David Thompson more than four years to reach Kettle Falls, just shy of halfway along the Columbia River from its source to its mouth. But even with all the halts he made on the lower section of the river, the remaining 1100 kilometres of travel — often into the headwinds for which the Columbia is notorious — required only 13 days. On one day, the brigade travelled 138 kilometres. The able voyageurs in the craft were not solely responsible. The pre-dammed Columbia, charged with a winter's worth of snowmelt, booted along at 16 kilometres per hour. The brigade also felt tidal effects — which would have added to their velocity on an ebb tide — as far as 225 kilometres upstream from the river's mouth. As the canoe flew down the river, Thompson took note of Mt. Hood and Mt. St. Helens. The antics of seals amused his men while the surveyor fretted over suspected damage to his sextant.

On the morning of July 15, the brigade came in sight of the Pacific Ocean. In his *Narrative,* Thompson recorded the clear distinction between the visionary at the helm, and the more narrow-minded voyageurs at the paddles. Above Tongue Point, on the Columbia River,

... brought us to a full view of the Pacific Ocean; which to me was a great pleasure, but my men seemed disappointed; they had been accustomed to the boundless horizon of the great lakes of Canada, and their high rolling waves; from the ocean they expected a more boundless view, a something beyond the power of their senses which they could not describe; and my informing them, that directly opposite us, at the distance of five thousand miles was the Empire of Japan added nothing to their ideas, but a map would.

Thompson's arrival at the mouth of the Columbia River was replete with as much fanfare as the circumstance and the remote situation would permit. Gabriel Franchère, a trader with the Pacific Fur Company (most of whose employees were Québecois), recorded the event in his journal.

> *Toward midday we saw a large canoe with a flag displayed at her stern, rounding … Tongue Point. We did not know who it could be … The flag she bore was British, and her crew was composed of eight Canadian boatmen or voyageurs. A well-dressed man, who appeared to be the commander, was the first to leap ashore; and addressing us without ceremony, he said that his name was David Thompson, and that he was one of the partners of the North West Company.*

Franchère was one of the new tenants of Fort Astoria, the recently constructed western outpost of the Pacific Fur Company. Franchère may have been surprised to see Thompson, but the NWC trader had expected to find the Americans at the mouth of the river. His notebook entry for July 10 concluded: "Hear news [from Natives] of the American ship's arrival."

The Americans received Thompson and his men politely, and Thompson reciprocated. But in his *Narrative* he expressed a dim view of the outpost, "which was four low log huts, the far famed Fort Astoria of the U.S." Thompson did not allow that his rivals were having a tough time. To command the *Tonquin*, Astor had settled on Jonathan Thorn, no captain, but an ex-U.S. Navy lieutenant widely regarded as a lunatic. When the *Tonquin* had arrived at the mouth of Columbia River three months earlier, by way of Hawaii, the crew was preparing to mutiny. The first five men that Thorn sent ashore promptly drowned when their boat capsized on the bar at the river's mouth. He ordered another craft put in and three more drowned. (It was to be at the same place and in the same manner that Alexander Henry the Younger would die, lost with seven others in a rowboat in 1814.)

To Duncan McDougall, in charge of Fort Astoria, Thompson gave a letter that outlined the agreement between the NWC and the Pacific Fur Company. It was not an official communication; Thompson whipped it up on the spot. Although neither trader knew that the deal had fallen through, they treated each other with a civil wariness. Each, in turn, attempted to discover the other's plans and motivations. This game of, "we are pleasantly surprised to see you/we are not at all surprised to see you," continued for a week, and was well summarized in a journal entry by Astoria trader, Alexander Ross.

> *For in point of acuteness, duplicity, and diplomatic craft, they [Thompson and McDougall] were perhaps well matched.*

Thompson's brief notebook entries during his stay at Fort Astoria are largely compass shots that record his survey of the complicated Columbia River estuary. He allowed that, "we hope to stay a few days to refresh ourselves." But the man who had just transformed most of a long-held dream into reality, boosted that accomplishment in his *Narrative.*

> *Thus I have fully completed the survey of this part*

of North America from sea to sea, and by almost innumerable astronomical observations have determined the positions of the mountains, lakes and rivers, and other remarkable places of the northern part of this continent; the maps of all of which have been drawn, and laid down in geographical position, being now the work of twenty-seven years.

In this passage Thompson attempts to make reaching the Pacific Ocean the climax of his story, but the proclamation falls shy of the truth. Thompson's survey of the Columbia River was far from complete; he was yet to acquaint himself with the 480 kilometre-long middle reach — almost one quarter of the river's length. This must have been on his mind when his brigade departed upstream on July 22, with three dugout canoes of a Pacific Fur Company brigade tagging along. It was a cat-and-mouse affair, each brigade wanting to see what the other had in mind. Thompson had told McDougall that he was going directly to Montréal. McDougall replied that his men were heading upstream to meet an overland brigade coming from St. Louis.

It would take Thompson 17 months to reach Montréal, and the Americans would soon build an outpost at the confluence of the Okanogan and Columbia rivers. The crews traded men. Thompson gave up voyageur Michel Boulard, whom he described as, "well versed in Indian affairs, but weak for the hard labor of ascending the river." In return he got a man from Hawaii, named Coxe. Thompson, as events and the river would prove, got a bargain.

Not far upriver, the Native people who earlier had been hospitable to Thompson became hostile and demanded payment for help with portaging. In one instance, Thompson brandished his pistol to thwart the attack of a dagger-wielding warrior. Soon after, Native warriors with poisoned arrows at the ready confronted the brigades at a portage. Thompson ordered his men to draw their pistols and muskets and to each take sight on one of the aggressors, with orders to fire if any warrior drew back on a bow string.

> *Coxe, the Sandwich Islander [Hawaiian], had marked out his man with his large pistol, which he held as steady as if it had been in a vice ... In this anxious posture we stood opposed to each other for full fifteen minutes, (it seemed a long half hour), when the upper rank began to break up, and in a few minutes the whole of them retired ...*

Thompson speculated that the change in the demeanor of the Native peoples was because the Americans were travelling unarmed, thus begging harassment. He added that this particular assembly of warriors had been without a chief, and thus acted as "bungling blockheads." Soon after these incidents, Thompson and the Americans parted.

Friendlier relations prevailed as Thompson's party moved upstream. Again he took time to stop and smoke with the local Native peoples. But travel was difficult. Camping places were few because of high water; one night his men slept standing up. The canoe leaked and the men could find no trees from which to procure gum or firewood. Everything was full of sand. The wind constantly blew a gale. But as always, even amid hardship, Thompson took note of the remarkable; in this case, a salmon 132 centimetres long.

At the confluence with the Snake River, Thompson decided to cut off the lower Big Bend of the Columbia. He turned east on the tributary. He sent a messenger ahead to Spokane House to ask Jaco Finlay to bring horses to a point on the Snake River, from where the brigade could head overland to the outpost. Jaco and the horses did not show up, so Thompson secured mounts from nearby Native people. The horse journey took only two days, but the men were again hungry, and resorted to butchering one of the recently purchased steeds. After six days at Spokane House, Thompson set off overland for Kettle Falls, which he reached in four days, on August 20. The Native people greeted him with a dance and presented Thompson with berries and dried salmon. The trader returned the kindness by laying down tobacco and, "other things to the amount of 32 skins" — a value of almost £16 — part of the cost of winning over the locals now that competition had arrived. It was September 2 before his men had crafted another cedar canoe, and had loaded it for the river.

Nestled within the greater epic of David Thompson's travels, the 17-day upstream journey on the middle reach of the Columbia River to Boat Encampment stands as one of its most energetic and risky episodes. A multitude of rapids — including the famed Dalles des Morts (Death Rapids) — all now quelled beneath reservoirs, would have demanded extreme skill and stamina. But the two manuscript pages of Thompson's *Narrative* that would have described this passage are missing. His notebooks record the courses, but little else. At one of the rapids — the Little Dalles, just north of present-day Revelstoke — a later traveller commented that it took two paddlers to maneuvre an otherwise empty canoe *downstream,* with seven more holding it by line from the bank. Thompson and his men lined, poled, and portaged their way through this section, passing two landmarks that had thwarted him on earlier travels — the mouths of the Pend Oreille and Kootenay rivers. On a beach near the Kootenay River's confluence with the Columbia River, Thompson saw caribou tracks. On September 7, he observed a comet in the evening sky.

The *Narrative* resumes after its missing pages with a beautiful account of how the Hawaiian, Coxe, became acquainted with snow.

> *He was for some time catching it [snow] in his hand, and before he could satisfy his curiosity it was melted; the next morning thin ice was formed, which he closely examined in his hand, but like the snow it also melted into water, and he was puzzled how the snow and ice could become water, but the great mountains soon settled his mind, where all became familiar to him.*

When he reached Boat Encampment, Thompson at last completed his survey of the Columbia River. He was expecting to find a brigade from east of the mountains, but no one was at the camp. After composing and posting a note describing his intentions, and taking a rest of just half an hour, Thompson made a curious decision to head upstream on the Canoe River. Ostensibly, he was looking for the brigade. In reality, he was probably taking advantage of a few "days off" in which to chart more territory. His party paddled to near the present-day site of Valemont, where a voyageur and a native guide, after having read the note, caught up with them. The supply brigade from the east had arrived at Boat Encampment. Thompson turned his craft around and shot the 77 kilometres to that camp in less than a day. There, William Henry informed the trader that the NWC was sending a man to replace him as head of the Columbia Department, so that Thompson might devote himself fully to surveying the route to the Pacific Ocean. It seems that even a bureaucracy as spare as that of the NWC was capable of assigning a person to a task after the task was completed.

It is difficult to conceive of the energy of David Thompson in 1811, who after such monumental journeys, totalling some 3300 kilometres, now set off on foot to cross Athabasca Pass, to help pack goods into a trading department for which he was no longer responsible. He returned to Boat Encampment by mid-October. After resting a week, Thompson set off once again, this time to make his only descent of the middle reach of the Columbia River. He delivered the trade goods to Spokane House, from where walked the 140 kilometres to the abandoned Saleesh House, arriving in mid-November.

It was as if David Thompson needed one more experience of the career that he had carved for himself: diplomat/surveyor/trader. He rebuilt the outpost and spent the winter trading with the Salish and Ktunaxa peoples, while filling blanks in his surveys of the Clark Fork and Flathead rivers. As a testament to how much the Native peoples respected Thompson, during a war council they sought his advice on whether they should make peace with the Piikani. He counselled them not to, unless they could strike a truce with every band of their enemy. On April 22, 1812, after more canoe building at Kettle Falls, David Thompson mustered an eastbound brigade and set off upstream on the Columbia River for the last time.

Epilogue

It is often said that David Thompson was the first to descend the Columbia River from its source to the Pacific Ocean. The surveyor never made a complete descent of the river — he travelled the section from Boat Encampment to the Blaeberry River only once, and that was upstream. Nor did he ever trace the river's entire course in a single journey. But by increments he did travel every reach of it, as well as sections of many of its tributaries.

A study of the river's course reveals the scope of this accomplishment. Because of the 14 dams on its main stem, the character of today's Columbia River is much different than it was in David Thompson's time. But the river is no less a riddle of hydrology. At various points along its length it flows to every direction on the compass. From its source at an elevation of 820 metres at Columbia Lake in southeastern B.C., the Columbia courses north for 305 kilometres between the Rockies and the Columbia Mountains before making an abrupt horseshoe around the north end of the Selkirk Mountains — a location known as Big Bend. It then flows south through the Arrow Lakes to where it receives one of its principal tributaries, the Kootenay River. Some

450 kilometres upstream of this confluence, the Kootenay River passes within two kilometres of Columbia Lake, but flows in the opposite direction to the Columbia River. This arrangement prompted one early commentator on the fur trade, Elliot Coues, to observe: "There are probably no other large rivers in North America whose interrelations are more peculiar than those which compose the system of upper Columbia waters."

Eight hundred kilometres from its source, the Columbia River crosses the Canada/U.S. border into Washington State at an elevation of 320 metres. In its upper reach, the river flows through inland rainforest; in eastern Washington the surroundings are virtually desert. The river trends south and then west, and then south and west again, as its makes for the Pacific Ocean. In its lower reach it has been diverted by lava flows and by glacial debris. As it chugs along the Washington/Oregon border, the river carves the basalt slot of the Columbia Gorge through the Cascade Mountains, before spilling into the sea.

When David Thompson began the easterly trek with the spring brigade from Boat Encampment on May 6, 1812, he left behind the Columbia River and, 10 days later, the mountains, forever. On the way east, he picked up Charlotte and family, including a son he had not met who was then more than a year old. When they arrived at Montréal in mid-August, Thompson was 42. He had not been in a city for more than 28 years. Since disembarking from the *Prince Rupert*, he had walked, snow-shoed, ridden, and canoed 88,550 kilometres, and had surveyed more than 3 million km^2 of wilderness. Apart from some mariners of the day, he had probably travelled farther than anyone else alive. Through all the trials, disasters, blunders, and triumphs of those travels, when he was in command of others, not a single member of his brigades had perished.

David Thompson's fame accrues from the first half of his life. But the man who had orchestrated a tremendous success in the wilderness never quite pulled things together in the civilized world. He settled with his family in Terrebone, just north of Montréal, with a guarantee of three years' returns on his NWC shares, and an annual compensation of £100 while he worked on his maps. Thompson initially drew at least two versions of his map of western North America. The first, completed in 1813, was shipped to Fort William, where it hung for 50 years in the great hall. This map contained one glaring error, the depiction of a fictitious Caledonia River, that lay between the courses of the Fraser and Columbia rivers, and which emptied into Puget Sound. The version of 1814 corrected the blunder, but the existence of the river was perpetuated for more than 40 years on pirated copies of the first map.

The 1814 map, glued together from 25 individual sheets, is just over three metres long and slightly over two metres high. It is displayed in a special cabinet at the Archives of Ontario in Toronto. Virtually intact after almost two centuries, the map is fading into wonderful hues of earthen sepia, dusky mauve, and misty magenta. This map was the defining document of Canadian cartography for a century. To stand before it is to marvel, to gain a true sense of the mind and the genius of David Thompson, and the breadth of the land that kindled that imagination. It is to come as close to touching history as the ancient art of a single person can make possible.

J.B. Tyrell, the geologist who purchased the manuscript of the *Narrative* from one of David Thompson's sons in 1889, saved the surveyor's story from being lost to the shoeboxes of history. Tyrell asserted that Thompson's record of his travels confirmed him, "in his rightful place as one of the greatest geographers of the world." But Tyrell also rendered a great disservice to his subject by attempting to place Thompson on another pedestal. Coupling Thompson's Christianity with his temperance, Tyrell stated that, "there were few white men in the West in those early days who bore so consistently as he did the white flower of a blameless life."

Tyrell chose to overlook aspects of Thompson's life that topple him from that moral pedestal. Thompson resisted trading liquor but was quick to trade muskets and ammunition. In his dealings with Natives and with rivals, he frequently resorted to duplicity. From his own correspondence, it is clear that Thompson fathered a child outside of, but probably before, his marriage to Charlotte. Present-day Salish Natives on the Flathead Reserve in Montana claim that descendants of David Thompson live among them, suggesting that Thompson was unfaithful to Charlotte during the winter of 1809–10. The surveyor advocated sending missionaries to convert Natives. His *Narrative* reveals a startlingly condescending tone: "It is doubtful if their language in its present simple state can clearly express the doctrines of Christianity in their full force." And there is the matter of Thompson's silence on pivotal events in 1810, his fabrication of that story in his *Narrative*, and his "missing notebook."

Thompson was evidently subject to ordinary human weaknesses. But if he was not a moral icon, he was certainly something else not lauded by Tyrell: an early individualist of national significance. An Englishman born of Welsh parents, Thompson worked for Scotsmen alongside companions who spoke either Québecois French or the myriad languages of First Nations. He was lame and half blind, and, at the time of his most important travels, was more interested in surveying than in reaping profits, yet he accomplished both. While others, notably Alexander Mackenzie and Simon Fraser, stormed off for the oceans in the quest for fame, Thompson dawdled in every watershed on his way from the Rockies to the Pacific Ocean, backtracking often, squinting at the stars while shivering, swatting skitters, and nearly starving. His modesty was genuine; in more than 26 years of travelling in the west, Canada's greatest explorer named a few landscape features for officials of the NWC, but did not drop a single name to commemorate himself or his men.

Epilogue

The poverty of Thompson's later years is a Canadian lament, but resulted as much from his own actions as from a lack of recognition. After his family moved to Glengarry, Upper Canada, he worked for the International (Canada/U.S.) Boundary Commission from 1815–26. During the last four years of his tenure he was the Commission's Chief Astronomer. Although his maps, and copies of them, were widely used, he received only a £150 settlement from the British government to acknowledge his contribution to the maps of Aaron Arrowsmith. The same government on two occasions declined to purchase a revised set of maps drawn between 1814–17. On its second appraisal of the maps, in 1843, the British foreign secretary stole the maps, which are still in London.

The NWC went bankrupt after a merger with the HBC in 1821, owing Thompson £400. The HBC subsequently castigated Thompson, perhaps in retaliation for his "desertion" 24 years earlier. He squandered some of his money on a failed housing scheme, on poor investments for his sons, and finally, on a foolish enterprise to supply wood to the British army. He was forced to sell his surveying equipment and even his coat to feed his family. In 1846, a doctor successfully treated him for cataracts. The following year, living with Charlotte at the house of one his daughters in Longueil, Lower Canada, he began work on his *Narrative.*

Canada's greatest surveyor and geographer is commemorated by four official Canadian place names: David

Thompson Lake in northern Ontario; Thompson Glacier in B.C.'s Cariboo Mountains; Mt. David, which overlooks the approach to Howse Pass in Alberta; and the Thompson River in B.C. (It was Simon Fraser who named the Thompson River, and David Thompson who named the Fraser River.) The name of Mt. David Thompson, in B.C.'s Premier Range, was changed to Mt. Sir John Thompson in 1927, to honour a Canadian Prime Minister. Six historic sites recall aspects of David Thompson's life: Rocky Mountain House, Kootanae House, Athabasca Pass, Henry House, a cairn near Castlegar, B.C., and Boat Encampment. There exists no known portrait or likeness of the surveyor made during his life.

David Thompson died on February 10, 1857 at age 86. Charlotte, although 15 years younger, died less than three months later. They are buried side by side at Mount Royal cemetery in Montréal, not far from Lachine, where the spring brigades put-in for the journey west.

Author's Notes

I have occasionally changed the unusual spelling, capitalization, and punctuation of material quoted from Thompson's *Narrative* and his notebooks to make the text more understandable. In places where Thompson used an abbreviation or omitted words, and the meaning might be unclear, I have added extra words or letters, enclosed by squared parentheses [ ].

The quoted material preserves the names that Thompson gave to First Nations. The present-day names and spellings preferred by First Nations follow in squared parentheses [ ]. Elsewhere in the text, I have used the present-day names preferred by First Nations. Canadian readers will know the Pend Oreille River as the Pend d'Oreille River, and the Okanogan River as the Okanagan River. U.S. readers will know the Kootenay River as the Kootenai River.

Bibliography

Henry, Alexander and David Thompson. *New Light on the Early History of the Greater Northwest; the Manuscript Journals of Alexander Henry, Fur Trader of the Northwest Company, and of David Thompson, Official Geographer and Explorer of the Same Company, 1799–1814*; Elliot Coues, editor. Minneapolis: Ross and Haines, reprint 1965.

Huck, Barbara, et al. *Exploring the Fur Trade Routes of North America.* Winnipeg: Heartland Associates Inc., 2002.

Jennings, John. *The Canoe, A Living Tradition.* Toronto: Firefly, 2002.

McCart, Joyce and Peter McCart. *On the Road With David Thompson.* Calgary: Fifth House Ltd., 2000.

Newman, Peter C. *Company of Adventurers.* Markham: Viking, 1985.

Newman, Peter C. *Caesars of the Wilderness.* Markham: Viking, 1987.

Bibliography

Nisbet, Jack. *Sources of the River, Tracking David Thompson Across Western North America.* Seattle: Sasquatch Books, 1994.

Ronda, James. *Astoria and Empire.* Lincoln: University of Nebraska Press, 1990.

Thompson, David. *Columbia Journals*; Barbara Belyea, editor. Montréal: McGill-Queen's University Press, 1994.

Thompson, David. *David Thompson's Narrative of his Explorations in Western North America, 1784–1812*; J.B. Tyrell, editor. Toronto: Champlain Society, 1916.

Thompson, David. *David Thompson's Narrative*; Richard Glover, editor. Toronto: Champlain Society, 1962.

Thompson, David. *Travels in Western North America, 1784–1812*; Victor G. Hopwood, editor. Toronto: Macmillan, 1971.

Acknowledgments

I thank the Champlain Society for making available on-line, its catalogue of works on Canadian history. I am grateful to authors Barbara Belyea, Elliot Coues, Jack Nisbet, and J.B. Tyrell, for their monumental work in transcribing David Thompson's notebooks. Kenton E. Spading of the U.S. Army Corps of Engineers, fielded questions concerning the source of the Mississippi River. Dr. Ian MacLaren, Department of History and Classics, and Department of English, at the University of Alberta, provided background information on Boat Encampment. Marnie Pole commented on the first draft of the story.

About the Author

Graeme Pole has hiked and skied a few of David Thompson's trails, and has canoed and kayaked reaches of the Columbia River. He is the author of one novel, and five non-fiction books that describe the human history and the natural history of the Canadian Rockies. Graeme and his family live near Hazelton in northwestern B.C., where he serves as a paramedic. Visit his website: www.mountainvision.ca

AMAZING STORIES™
HUDSON'S BAY
COMPANY ADVENTURES
The Rollicking Saga of Canada's Fur Traders
HISTORY
by Elle Andra-Warner

HUDSON'S BAY COMPANY ADVENTURES

The Rollicking Saga of Canada's Fur Traders

"Suddenly, out of the silent night — KABOOM! — a cannon shot fired through the house, passing under the servant's arm. Before anyone could react, another cannon shot flew in front of Mrs. Sergeant's face. She fainted. The French commandos had arrived. Fort Albany was under attack."

This sizzling, action-packed account of Canada's riotous early days recounts the schemes and schemers that launched a famous trading empire. From its earliest days, the Hudson's Bay Company battled everyone and everything just to survive. History not for the faint of heart!

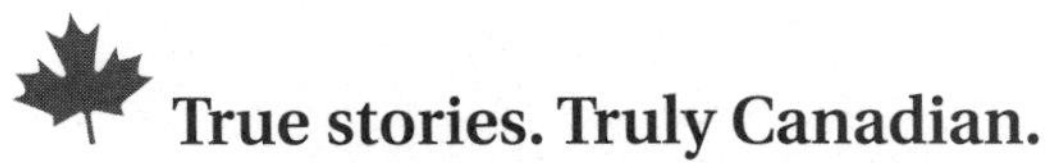

ISBN 1-55153-958-6

EARLY VOYAGEURS

The Incredible Adventures of the Fearless Fur Traders

"The trips they undertake, the strains they endure, the dangers to which they are exposed, and... the efforts they have to make, all of this defies the imagination."

Francois-Xavier de Charlevoix, Missionary

For more than 200 years, voyageur canoes charged across the waters from Quebec to British Columbia, and north to Hudson Bay. Spending months at a time in the backwoods, braving dangerous rapids, and portaging over rough terrain, the voyageurs were the epitome of tough, rugged adventurers.

True stories. Truly Canadian.

ISBN 1-55153-970-5

AMAZING STORIES

ALSO AVAILABLE!

MARIE-ANNE LAGIMODIÈRE

The Incredible Story of Louis Riel's Grandmother

" Marie-Anne, seven months pregnant, would have to travel 50 kilometres on horseback. Unfazed, she set off with [a baby] hanging from one side of the saddle in her moss bag, balanced by a bag of provisions on the other side. "

Marie-Anne Lagimodière was a force to be reckoned with. Her honeymoon was a four-month journey from Quebec to Pembina with a brigade of tough voyageurs. She criss-crossed Canada with her fur trader husband during the early 1800s. Her legacy is enormous. Within 10 years of her death, at the ripe old age of 95, she already had more than 630 direct descendants including Louis Riel, the Métis leader.

ISBN 1-55153-967-5